Loose Cannons

RECENCIES

Recencies Series: Research and Recovery in Twentieth-Century American Poetics
Matthew Hofer, Series Editor

This series stands at the intersection of critical investigation, historical documentation, and the preservation of cultural heritage. The series exists to illuminate the innovative poetics achievements of the recent past that remain relevant to the present. In addition to publishing monographs and edited volumes, it is also a venue for previously unpublished manuscripts, expanded reprints, and collections of major essays, letters, and interviews.

ALSO AVAILABLE IN THE RECENCIES SERIES:

How Long Is the Present: Selected Talk Poems of David Antin edited by Stephen Fredman

Amiri Baraka and Edward Dorn: The Collected Letters edited by Claudia Moreno Pisano

The Shoshoneans: The People of the Basin-Plateau, Expanded Edition by Edward Dorn and Leroy Lucas

Loose Cannons

Selected Prose

Christopher Middleton

Foreword by
August Kleinzahler

University of New Mexico Press | Albuquerque

© 2014 by the University of New Mexico Press
All rights reserved. Published 2014
Printed in the United States of America
19　18　17　16　15　14　　1　2　3　4　5　6

LIBRARY OF CONGRESS CATALOGING-IN-PUBLICATION DATA

Middleton, Christopher, 1926–
 [Poems. Selections]
 Loose cannons : selected prose / Christopher Middleton.
　　pages ; cm — (Recencies Series: Research and Recovery in Twentieth-Century American Poetics)
 ISBN 978-0-8263-5519-5 (pbk. : alk. paper) — ISBN 978-0-8263-5520-1 (electronic)
 I. Title.
 PR6025.I25A6 2014
 821'.914—dc23
　　　　　　　　2014002209

Cover art courtesy of *Philip Trussell*
Book design by *Lila Sanchez*
Composed in *Balzano and Minion Pro*

Contents

Foreword by August Kleinzahler — vii
Prologue by Christopher Middleton — ix

1

Curbaram — 3
The Birth of the Smile — 5
From the Alexandria Library Gazette — 7
Manuscript in a Lead Casket — 12
A Bachelor — 19
Ignorance — 23
A Memorial to the Room-Collectors — 26
Nine Biplanes — 38

2

Or Else — 45
Louise Moillon's Apricots (1635) — 49
From *Serpentine*
  Ingestion — 54
  This Is Lavender — 57
  The Green Heron — 59
  Commodus — 60
  Fruit Bringers — 67
Bivouac — 71
The Image — 74

3

From Earth Myriad Robed	77
The Turkish Rooftops	86
The Execution of Maximilian	92
Balzac's Face	94
Cliff's Dwarf	96
Le Déjeuner	99
In the Mirror of the Eighth King	103

4

Coriolan	107
Parthenogenesis in Charcoal	111
A Polka in the Evening of Time	113
The Gaze of the Turkish Mona Lisa	115
A Postscript to the Great Poem of Time	121
From *Depictions of Blaff*	
The Pines of Rome	124
The Sycorax Syndrome	126
The Weathervane Oiler	131
Thoreau's Arrow	134

Sources and Notes   137

Foreword

These thirty-three *prose inventions* of Christopher Middleton constitute the fourth pillar of an extraordinary literary oeuvre, the other three being his poetry, translations, and literary essays, each a singular achievement in its respective genre, and each in its way informing the *prose inventions*, or *imaginative prose*, or what Middleton himself would refer to as "short prose." Whatever one chooses to call these often astonishing miniatures, they are certainly Middleton's wildest, most accessible, and most entertaining work and count as some of his very finest writing.

These prose pieces travel somewhere amid the realms of fable, parable, meditation, brief life, character portrait, anecdote, and dreamscape. The mind at work, or more properly put, at play, in these pieces resists categorization, almost by its nature and the nature of its undertaking. Though Middleton, in his own writing on the short prose form, refers to its "subversive" and "ludic force," its "animular miniaturism," by which he means *animated* in a very particular sense (deriving from Paracelsus), where revery and animation mix in a kind of hypnogogic condition to produce heightened imaginative and unexpected constructs in miniature. *Subversive* and *ludic*, along with *liminal* and *disruptive*, are his favored terms in describing the kinds of literature which most engage him.

Middleton identifies certain examples of the short prose form he himself works within as "perspectival antigrams" and "metaphysical cliffhangers," for that latter citing, among other works, Franz Kafka's "An Imperial Message" and Jorge Luis Borges' "Parable of Palace." His own inventions, in their distinctive methods and tonalities, echo those two authors as well as scores of others, including Kenneth Patchen, Alfred Jarry in his *'pataphysical* forays, and Robert Walser in his short prose.

Here is Middleton, from his "Introduction to an Unpublished Anthology of Short Prose":

The animular miniaturism of short prose . . . secretes a subversive force . . . as well, a ludic [playful] force. Its loophole procures views, in anomalous perspectives, upon worlds, often vast, other and complex. Its ludic character, sifting from the billow of language a few aleatory particles, may also align those particles in such a way as to suggest tensions at large in universal life. . . . Some modern short prose writings, too, insofar as they gainsay predictable literary conventions . . . might be called perspectival antigrams. These are enigmas or metaphysical cliff-hangers. . . . In the pregnancy of these antigrams, a naive attention of curiosities of nature, as to outlandish freaks of behavior . . . has been interiorized and subtilized into crystalline intelligence fathoming its language at outer limits of the imaginable.

These prose pieces reveal the illuminating power of "lyrical imagination"—a subject Middleton has written on brilliantly and in depth—understood as a "wild free particle," one that is resistant by definition to being "contained" and, quoting Loren Eiseley, enjoys "the rare freedom of the particle to do what most particles never do."

By which Middleton means, I think, to actively discover *places* or *moments* outside the customary or habituated orbits of traditional literary practice, *places* and *moments* charged by the primal and unpredictable sources of lyrical expression, be it short, imaginative prose or poetry or birdsong. In order to get there, or be available to those root impulses, during the course of which one deciphers the "code in which the nervous system expresses itself while communing with the world" involves a kind of struggle or dance of the "mind straining against horizons which the will imposes."

The serious reader will have an exhilarating time of it tracking Middleton's "dance of the intellect" (to use Pound's term) as he *strains* with his own, very particular, fierce delight against those same horizons.

—August Kleinzahler

Prologue

In view of its worldwide flourishing for the last sixty years or so, it should by now be recognized that "short prose" differs from the short story and the prose poem. Even then, due to its dynamics and varieties, short prose is not easy to pin down categorically. Its sources, too, are many. Just think of *Gesta Romanorum*, of writings by John Earle and of Ben Jonson, of Pascal, of character portraits and aphorisms, of the extraordinary Lichtenberg—all the way to Kafka, to Kenneth Patchen's *Aflame and Afun of Walking Faces*.

The germ of short prose has probably been in a constant interior metamorphosis, even allowing for pressure from time and milieu. We could think of it as a resistance to the tendency of written prose to prolong itself, to expand. How obvious, but it brings us to the concept of an antigram, a variety of imaginative writing which revolts against and may reverse the programmatic. I discover grounds enough for thinking that short prose should enshrine something not-said, a hiatus, a vestige of mystery—"Many a fervent and delicate friendship has been devastated by the opening of a rose" (Chamfort).

The germ grows, as it must. The art of short prose would then provide for its keeping its "vestige of mystery" more or less in evidence. The antigram calls for (and should arouse) the most scrupulous thrift, panache, and refinement in writing as such. Beautiful shafts of short prose (Russian, Polish, German) have galled the political police. In its narrative form it has condensed the histories of South America.

It is from such speculation about this secret genre, which lurks between the paving stones of established literary discourse, that my workings took their departure. Few enough are really short; beauty is exuberance.

—Christopher Middleton

1

Curbaram

Curbaram says: At present they are encamped outside the walls, and we shall drive them back into the city. From this hill you can count their horses, unsaddled, in the enclosure to the left, also their tents, including the storage tents, which are not round but square. One thousand four hundred and thirty-two men spread over an area of one mile: by eleven thirty they will be concentrated at the city gate, a tumultuous mass of armour, horses, elbows and heavy feet. At that time you will stop firing and save your ammunition. They will kill one another as they try to press through the gate. By noon we shall have them inside the walls, and they will see us, crowding these ridges with our camels and artillery. The rocket batteries will be positioned at these three points, northwest, south and east of the city. You will maintain a heavy and constant fire from shortly after noon until the sun sets.

Some of these men will plan to escape from the city after nightfall. They will lower ropes from the parapets, and arrive at the foot of the west wall one half hour after midnight. Probably they will be called Guillaume, Albric and Wido, but you need not concern yourselves with that: besides, there will be others, of whose names I am not yet certain. Well now, these men, about twenty in number, having reached the foot of the wall, will move stealthily westwards, making for the sea. The terrain is not easy. By three thirty their exhausted boots will have given up on them, the soles torn away by the rocks which carpet the entire area west of the city to within half a mile of the sea shore. They will continue to move forward barefoot, then on their hands and knees. By dawn, their hands, feet and knees will be lacerated down to the bones, but they will keep moving, for at dawn they will, at last, get a first sight of the ships. The ships are manned by their own people, sailors from Akra Korakas, Archangel, Florida and Plymouth. Then they will be standing, kneeling and lying on the shore, perhaps even feeling the sea as it cools their wounds and stings their eyes. At that moment, the sailors will up-anchor and cram on sail, for they will be subjected to a concerted attack by our air and sea forces: the galleys from coves north of Port Saint Simeon, carrying archers and cannon, and aircraft loaded with bundles of our widely read literature. The ships will attempt to escape, while they, for their part, will stand on the shore, shouting and waving and weeping with the pain of their wounds and their worstedness. Their ships will consequently be destroyed, as soon as their sailors have seized the opportunity to study our discharged literature.

The men on the shore will then retreat to the low dunes, where, human strength being not easily exhausted in times of stress, they will build a defensive wall of sand, rocks, seaweed and rotten fish. The wall will be fifteen yards long, three and a half feet tall, and two feet wide. It may, even at noon, provide them with a modicum of shade.

The Birth of the Smile

There are three legends about the birth of the smile, each relating to a different epoch. It is the custom to tell these legends in a reverse chronological sequence, as if this might hopefully point toward an ever-receding antiquity with secrets which may one day be told in legends that still have to be discovered.

The first legend concerns the Sumerians. These people came down from the mountains to the plains, in search of food and water. After several centuries of food and water they became bored with the flatness of the plains, pined for the ancient exertion of striding up and down mountains, and decided to build a mountain of their own (there could be no question of returning to the old place). For ten years the men laboured at the mountain. It was the priests who put the finishing touches to it—drilling weeper-holes, planting a tree on top, fashioning chambers inside, near the base, for library materials and, inevitably, a toilet. While the priests were getting busy, an enormous sheet, woven during these ten years by the women, was draped around the mountain. Finally, everyone assembled; and then the mountain was unveiled with due ceremony and with a great beating of gongs. As the sheet sank to the ground, the strings having been cut by some excessively large pairs of Sumerian scissors, the mountain stepped fresh and naked out of its veilings, and all the Sumerians smiled for the first time. This was a short smile, all the same. The

Sumerians had built a mountain to walk up and down, a mountain of the heart, a mountain of despair, a mountain of pain; but their smile disappeared when the officiating priest, from under the tree at the top, declared: "This place is a holy place; for whom it is intended, do not ask. And do not enter or climb around on the outside either, or you will die."

The second legend tells that the smile was born on the face of the first woman when she stood for the first time before the first man and perceived the silence with which his phallus grew and rose at the pleasure of her presence.

The third legend tells of an epoch which must have preceded that of the second, if only by a few days. This is what the legend says. When the shaper of life was making men and women, he was careful to give them strong contours to contain the spirit in them. There was always the danger that these forms might dissolve into the flowing which goes through all things. The spirit raged in the new beings, wrathful at being contained, and after mighty strainings and heavings it burst out in fire. The fire streamed from the bodies of the creatures and all creation might have been consumed, had it not been for a cool god who took the spirit in hand. Suddenly he was standing there, in front of a girl. As they faced each other, an island of coolness was created in the midst of the burning. As he gazed at the girl, he began to marvel at her lightness and grace, and at the diaphanous body from which the fire was spreading in great lashes. The god spoke divine words to her body, as he gazed in wonder. While he was speaking, the spirit overheard these words and for the first time began to grow content in such a dwelling. That was when the girl smiled. In those times, a smile was simply the consent of the spirit to dwell in us.

If older legends are ever discovered, they may explain to us the terrified smile of Kafka; or the smile inserted at the corners of Che Guevara's mouth by the thumbs of his murderers.

From the Alexandria Library Gazette

The story goes that Aeschylus was killed by a blow on the head from a tortoise dropped by an eagle. Included in the story is a supposition that the eagle, mistaking the bald head of Aeschylus for a stone, had dropped the tortoise in order to break its shell. The case is unusual; who can tell, it may be unique. In our time there is small chance of anyone, let alone a distinguished playwright, dying in such an original way. Even in those stirring times when young men could easily remember the moment when as toddlers they heard the news that the Persians had been defeated, the event might have caused a ripple of concern. Yet there is only one version of the story in our library at Alexandria. The absence of any variant versions, quite apart from the oddity of the event itself, offers ground for suspicion. One might even say: the report itself is unique, but the case is reminiscent of thousands.

It is possible that Aeschylus was deported and the story invented by an official to cover up the event. We know that the playwright had been in court, on at least one occasion, to answer charges of impiety. Also it is said that his face betrayed the greatest ferocity while he was composing. Deportation and exile, for such a patriot as Aeschylus, who had been in the thick of it at Marathon and Plataea, would have entailed a death hardly less rapid than any induced by a blow on the head from a tortoise. Or, to amplify the field of doubt somewhat, he might indeed have been killed by such a blow, only by a blow from a tortoise dropped, or swung, by an official, whose action would thus have made exile superfluous. Speculate as one may, the case calls for disinterested inquiry. Who knows, the story may have been fabricated to mask a crime; its author, too, uneasy in an imposed official role, may have known what actually occurred but in the circumstances could go no further than issue an explanation which, if times became less turbulent, might somewhere prompt the raising of a reasonable eyebrow.

Certain attendant facts should be taken into account. Let us assume that the story matches the event. In view of the fact that Aeschylus possessed only one hand (he had lost the other at Salamis while boarding a Persian warship), he might have had less chance to defend himself against a falling tortoise than a man with two hands— presuming, be it said, that the tortoise could have emitted some kind of warning signal, whistling through the air, casting a shadow that grew ever larger as its body approached the head. On such grounds the event, though improbable, is not impossible. Another fact is Aeschylus' reputed ferocity. He could, for instance, have been composing, could have seen overhead an eagle flying with a tortoise in its beak, have dropped his pen across the page, a mass of deletions and doodles, pushed back his chair and rushed ferociously from his atelier, an open-air atelier, very pleasant in the Greek springtime, when tortoises are fresh and abundant, have shouted "That's for me!" and, running as fast as his legs could carry him, a spry man at sixty-nine, though bald, have followed the flight of the eagle across pastures and possibly vineyards—he drank copiously, it is said, while composing—until he stood directly under the eagle, whereupon the tortoise, released as the eagle opened its beak in astonishment at finding such a convenient shining stone, or even at sighting such an active human being, fell and struck.

Even if these were not the actual phases of the event, one might boldly suggest that in the last phase, seeing to his exasperation that the tortoise was going to miss him by inches, Aeschylus raised the leathery stub of his left wrist and deflected the falling body sufficiently for it to strike his skull without loss of momentum or impact. Such a death would indeed not ill befit a poet whose ferocity, in his declining years, might have turned against his own person; whose imagination was, as they say, fruitful in prodigies; who actually had moved his household to the country, being sick of city life; and whose fate it was to have composed ninety dramatic works of which only seven have been handed down to us.

Yet a problem does remain. Who saw this happening? Or, since it is the factual basis of the story that is in doubt, who found the tortoise and the playwright in such close proximity that some foul causal relation between the two might be suspected? Supposing that someone did find the tortoise lying close to Aeschylus with his fatal skull fracture, was this person identical with the person who established, for all time, the causal relation? If so, we might impugn his good sense. Conceivably, indeed quite probably, this person did not see an eagle. He may have done, or he may have glimpsed a flying object which he supposed to be an eagle; but that lesser likelihood can be touched on later. For the present, we can imagine that someone finds playwright and tortoise, also blood, possibly bone splinters, on the shell of the tortoise. But how did he fail to observe that the juxtaposition might be explained very simply as follows: Aeschylus, out walking, captures a tortoise and is taking it home for supper, for eventual soup, or even for a child to play with, when along comes a bandit, who attacks Aeschylus, with a view to wresting from his one hand the still animate tortoise, strikes Aeschylus with the tortoise, which might also have been a fair dish for a bandit, but runs away in terror, now spurning the tortoise on account of its being bespattered with blood and bone splinters. The bandit, be it conjectured, might also have been an official, whose function was to shadow Aeschylus when he went for walks. Such an official might also have received instructions to wait for the right moment; and the tortoise, for a Greek in those days, could well have been in his view the very image of the right moment: one can never be sure if it is coming or going anywhere.

Be that as it may, the person might actually have seen the whole episode, with eagle dropping tortoise, with or without Aeschylus accelerating across pasture and vineyard and finally halting at the momentous spot. Indeed, the person might have witnessed just such an event as is reported in the story. But it is unlikely that this should be the case. For one thing, eagles do not carry tortoises through the sky, but devour them where they catch them, carefully pecking out the insides with a long and suitably hooked beak. For another, an eagle would not fly with a tortoise, granting for a moment that it might for some personal reason have been flying with one at all, so high as to be unable to distinguish between a bald head and a stone below. Thirdly, if the eagle might conceivably be going to the trouble of transporting through the air a tortoise of magnitude sufficient for a meal, then it would also take the trouble to keep its beak firmly closed on whatever extension of the tortoise it had contrived to take hold of. An eagle could have been sighted, but its relation to the dropped tortoise, or to the swung tortoise, is a question not to be settled without careful reference to the known facts of aquiline behaviour.

The problem remains: even with reference to the known facts of aquiline behaviour the question cannot be settled. What is said to have happened could have happened, and it could also not have happened. The story, if it is a fabulation, might conceal a horrible truth. Or the death itself might have been, in conformity with Aeschylus' cast of mind, horribly fabulous. So it stands, like many of the messages reaching us from ages past: bold, clear, and inscrutable.

The elementary components of the story—head, eagle, and tortoise—glitter but dazzle us like crystals held up to the sun. We tend to read them as cryptic symbols, not as a faithful or literal recording of events. What creatures we are of our climate of suspicion. Thus the eagle, whose domain is the sky, cracks the head, which is located between earth and sky, with a tortoise, a creature like ourselves quite shiftlessly terrestrial. Is there a narrator here, giving the world a coded account of some crime, or even a laughable saga about some frightful conflict crystallizing in the mind of Aeschylus as he walked in the countryside, a conflict which induced his death with or without help from an eagle and a tortoise? Or did the events narrated occur and was this pattern of events itself a spontaneous epiphany of some collision of incompatibles occurring in Aeschylus' head? Such fables can, indeed, spring out of nature herself, concocted by her obscure demands and composed in her own signs, while some more or less corruptible witness with a human look stands by to welcome her dictation. Even then, what a calamitous end for a playwright peering into the sizeable gap between earth and heaven, men and gods. Killed like a rabbit. Whoever can have been so cruel as to teach Aeschylus such a lesson, seeing that it was scheduled for the moment when the tortoise smashed his skull. Even if the tortoise was swung by an official, while an eagle flew indifferently overhead, what a brutal last message for an explorer of the ways between us and them.

Another detail, seldom mentioned, refers us to the question of the oracles. An oracle had predicted that Aeschylus would be killed by a falling house. Accordingly, he went to the country, where, in his time, houses were fewer and farther between. So it might look as if he had been willing to survive, for the time being. There, however, in the country, the tortoise struck him as it fell, giddy no doubt, but still ensconced in its mobile house of tortoise shell. As the vulgar might say: he had it coming to him in any case. Yet here, too, there might have been a trick. These oracles—on rare occasions they were bought by the higher officials; perhaps in this case somebody had wanted Aeschylus to move, under no apparent compulsion, to a place where his demise would not be observed by neighbours, cleaning women, and the rest. His assassin must have indeed been possessed by the demon of analogy when he recognized, in the tortoise, the right weapon and the right moment, and when he saw, or did not see, an eagle appositely floating by.

Manuscript in a Lead Casket

The sight of that grinning rubberized plastic troll, up for sale among certain other anthropological oddities, has brought back to my mind in a flash the entire story of Tourist City. Everyone is familiar with the primitive stages: the annual invasions of coastal regions, the empty islands filling overnight with swarms of people, old cities bustling with foreign widows greedy for adventure, the streams of trains, ships, airplanes, and cars transporting in all directions, come the summer, hosts of strangers who had borrowed, won, or earned enough to take a trip. Industries blossomed to cater for these sporadic migrants. Objects were created to please and to pacify them, for all wished to return home displaying some novelty as evidence that they had been somewhere. All these strangers were alike in one way: what they were doing was only provisional. And for many it was a pleasure to get home again and back to the routine, in this profession or that, able to brew one's own tea in one's own kitchen, and so on. I do not speak of other multitudes who, for reasons of poverty or other disadvantaged circumstances brought on by oppression, were never to know the delights, or the torments, of tourism. The secular holiday was, of course, an institution created by the urban middle class of an even earlier epoch; rapidly it became a ritual of ventilation, as that class became stuffier and stuffier. Early in our period, the mass of these migrants became so numerous that the ritual lost all efficacy, just as pilgrimages once, in simpler times, having first woven the lively fabric of commerce and community, gradually came to abandon their sacred objectives. No place remained fresh or strange, no stranger stood fast in originality.

Yet a new situation did arise, and the history of tourism took another turn, with the appearance in Denmark one day of a gentleman named J. Heilbut. For in Heilbut's passport there were some entries of an unusual character, *viz.*, his nationality was given as Tourist, and his profession likewise. Not only was J. Heilbut the first professional Tourist national; he was also the first up-to-date inspector of tourist accommodations, commodities, and travel facilities. In his suitcase he carried a rubber stamp, which he employed with discrimination. With this rubber stamp he established, once and for all, the mediocrity of products, places, and so forth, with a flourish that made all previous inscriptions, plaquettes, badges and listings look thoroughly quaint. A guarantee of mediocrity from J. Heilbut was the wildest dream of hoteliers, grand or small, likewise of the manufacturers of transportable tourist objects. It meant the certainty of business, it meant that such accommodations, or such products, had been admitted into the pattern of total uniformity which the demon Tourism had decreed to be ideal. After all, nobody by now wanted the hardship of adjusting, for such a short while, to a different mode of life; nobody, either, wanted to know if a product was good, so long as his main intent was to value it according to where it had come from.

J. Heilbut's career was an interesting one, but I shall not dwell on it. The effects which it produced on tourism as a whole by far exceeded his singular, often lonely, always courageous efforts to bring relief into a suffocated traveller's world. Probably the most momentous of these effects was the construction of the aforementioned Tourist City, a task, nay, an achievement which combined the energy of a Michelangelo with the inventiveness of a Leonardo, and, perhaps, the panache of a Benvenuto Cellini. J. Heilbut's paper "Turismo y Weltschicksal," which he read at the Fourth Tourist International, contained the first germs of such a conception. There, characteristically, he wrote: "We need a centre where all can find what they seek. We must construct a dome of many-coloured immemorial brass. These multitudes, why must they always be going somewhere, with their suitcases and stomach aches? Let us gather together the scattered members in one Great Good Place."

Below me lies that City, bathed in its medley of illuminations, overhead the crescent moon, casting a faint beam or two upon the distant beaches and the sea which laps the shores of this artificial island. The museums are closed, sombre medieval streets run crisscross over the underground computer section, with its pressure chambers, the Tower of London flanking Red Square and floodlit on my right. Let me explain, as they say. But I must be brief. Gradually the monuments were gathered here and reconstructed under expert supervision. The city area can be crossed on foot inside seventy-five minutes, if you do not stop to admire anything. The Western Sector is dominated by the Vatican, complete with Swiss Guards and an authentic Pope; around it are placed, within easy walking distance, the Luxembourg Gardens, two hundred yards of Borobodur, and the Soviet Palace of Athletes. Bernini's original approach to the Vatican, meanwhile, is intersected by the numerous aforementioned medieval streets, which were plucked from the hearts of various towns, *viz.*, Sospel, Carcassonne, Prague, and even Newcastle (the Morden Tower street). These alleys are paved with original cobblestones, and donkeys may be hired for a fee, imitating the custom at Clovelly. Here, too, the Quick Ruin can be seen. This was a later addition, introduced after complaints that a tour of the city was still a long haul. The Quick Ruin has proved to be a strong attraction, especially for provincials from Kiev and Kansas. Litter may be purchased with your ticket, for disposal among the romanesque fonts and Greek friezes. The Northern Sector is dominated by Venice—not the whole of Venice, to be sure, only the area from the Rialto bridge down to and including Saint Mark's and the Campo San Marco as well (minus the dock areas beyond, also the Doge's Palace simply could not be budged). The acquisition of this area was extremely difficult and tedious, but the venal Venetians were eventually swayed by some promises. The same area contains a wing of the Louvre, the Paddington Canal (not much of the Grand Canal could be spared), some parts of Taxco and Krk, and the Sun Pyramid from Chichen Itza. Underground, a concession to visitors whose dada is archaeology, a complete replica of the gigantic Mas d'Azil Cavern has been installed, with some stuffed bears in the entrance chamber, to give a genuine touch. Again above-ground are placed several fields, with buttercups, a small Dorset vale, and two dells from the vicinity of Zug (cf. Wilhelm Tell). The whole sector is popular with nature lovers (its climate is controlled); but it offers much to linguists as well. It is perhaps the foremost *site pittoresque classé*, while the Western Sector contains the foremost *ville pittoresque moyenâgeuse*.

To the east of Krk lies the Roman Forum, which in turn is the access to a seventeenth-century Bohemian castle. Thus we arrive in the Eastern Sector, with its splendid Pillars of Memnon, erected outside a group of cafés where salaried writers and intellectuals may be overheard as they discuss the works of their colleagues. This area has again proved quite popular, especially among students who, bright-eyed, taperecord the dialogues for incorporation into their research projects. The sector also houses the resident Viennese whores, whose sumptuous looks and lively language attract all comers, even dialectologists. They are generally to be found in the Amical Bar, or in the Self-Service Autosnack, but some cling to their original haunt, the Mikado. The Tower of Pisa is here, too, and, one of the great scientific accomplishments of the City Executive, a regular and immense supply of Italian smell and noise from all kinds of motorized vehicles (driven, or ridden, needless to say, by a grinning host of papagallos and some Mexicans).

The Southern Sector provided many headaches for the Executive. It was decided that the sector should be devoted chiefly to Views. It is a historical fact that tourists need Views, indeed they have been figuring in the manuals since the eighteenth century. But how to provide the Views? How could the Grand Canyon possibly be uprooted, or a glacier from the Pamirs? This mechanical problem harrassed the planners for two years. Eventually a senior psychologist found the answer: people do not want the Views, they want photographs of them, preferably with a relative, friend, self, or goat, occupying the foreground. Here, then, was the breakthrough. The sector is devoted to the sale and purchase of postcards showing Views with persons in the foreground (with goats, mules, squirrels, or pigeons provided as company, if desired). But, even more, this Reproduction Sector, as it came to be called, spawned in time a quantity of shops, stalls, boutiques, booths, and machines, for the vending of novelties. The novelties are not Views, to be sure, but they are, as it were, concentrated concrete samples of the most various forms of base optical experience: vulgarized Views, if you like, myopic Views, degenerate Views, as the following select list of items may serve to show:

miniature wooden man with corkscrew penis
permanent bottle-cork with head of General de Gaulle
plastic Greek nude with protective girdle
various pictures of Petrarch's tomb
tiny tight pink sack of lavender
goose (with goslings) in milky blue glass two centimetres long
pink plastic baby peeing into pot inscribed Souvenir of Venice
miniature Chac Mool in solid brown plastic
stereotype oval miniature of Lorenzo Medici
defecating Bavarian peasant holding wicker fruit basket
black and yellow painted pottery cicada from Provence
plastic bust of Julius Caesar
model gondola, black and white, with cabin amidships and ballerina
    on prow dancing to tune from musical box (Tchaikovsky)
photos of popes
balsawood doll-sunshade with pretty inscription
seventeen varieties of key ring with emblazoned leather tongue
model plastic Vatican with interior light bulb and inbuilt Ave Maria
    musical box
dolls in colourful national costume inside tubular cellophane boxes

Stetson hats
Gregorian antiphon on genuine parchment
one hundred and fourteen varieties of plastic handbag
yellowed plaster Venus head with curly hairdo and becomingly
    broken nose
rings chains bangles lockets brooches in various perishable metals
snowfall paperweight enclosing famous monument
roughly stitched model bull in imitation ratskin on pedestal

    I list these items with emotion, for the singular does invest such objects with a kind of dignity, though in fact the opposite is the case: they come and they go, like the tourists themselves, in their identical disposable millions. In this Southern Sector, too, stands the Institute of Place History, located appropriately in the basement of the White House. Here favourite tourist travelogues on tape, pickings from all the most mendacious guidebooks, have fully supplanted the obsolete monographs by local scholars, eccentrics, and trained observers. The taped travelogues may also be obtained in Tourese, the international tourist language, whose vogue began with the influx of Japanese brides into California, Norway, and Chinese Turkestan. Beauty contests for Miss Tourist are held weekly between the Pillars of Memnon, only a stone's throw from the Wailing Wall, now used for the hanging of art shows (the Genuine Oil Spanish Dancer is always a sell-out). The school for tourism, on the other hand, is located in the Western Sector, actually in the Vatican. Where else would one properly begin the mental voyage toward a diploma in Tourist Theatrics, including the highest and lowest modalities of Camp?

    My time is short, I have sketched the dispositions of Tourist City, which is now in its sixth flourishing year, and for which additions in plenty are under way. As for me, I was forgotten long ago; here I have lived my last months, unquestioned, unsuspected. Yet my work is not forgotten, would that it were. The investigations of my earlier days were nothing but the logical development of tendencies set in motion many years before. Out of this logical development emerged unerringly what I do now call, without hesitation, a nightmare. In my frail old hands, however, I hold the charm which shall awaken this dreamer. Read the spell backwards I cannot. But I can perform, and shall perform, the act which was being prepared, for all I know, behind all my endeavours since that day of destiny in Denmark. This act is to destroy the entire city. I have worked secretly for months, setting the charges in the pressure chambers, placing the fuses, bringing the leads underground to this abandoned Venetian palace, from whose highest window I shall send out into the night these words. In a few moments, everything will be blown to pieces. I too, J. Heilbut, shall find in that destruction a kind of justice.

A Bachelor

I am deeply perplexed about three things: my mother, my girl friend, and my room. Perhaps I am not capable of being as deeply perplexed as I should be; perhaps I am incapable of depth. I know what some people think they mean when they talk of depth. On the other hand, my mother, my girl friend, and my room, are as perplexing to me as I could wish.

My mother suffers from nocturnal regurgitations and wishes to be an Italian. My girl friend must be mad, she goes out at night (when she is here, also when she is not here, I suppose) and rescues all kinds of rubbish from the streets. As for my room, it is spacious and pleasant, but I have a compulsion to avoid noticing it: where am I?

My mother is fairly old now, but not childish. She is a healthy person, in most ways, and the nocturnal regurgitations are her only affliction, apart from a tendency to speak excitedly about everyday things. She does not read metaphysics, otherwise I might find it in me to suppose that her nocturnal regurgitations are caused by something other than stomach acid. As for her wish to be Italian, that is understandable. Even at her age she knows the attraction of the antithesis. She has been to Italy twice, and on each occasion (with an interval of forty years between the first and the second) she has been thrown into paroxysms of joy by trivial things, the eating of an orange or a doughnut, the politeness of an old man (he a widower, she a widow) who opened a gate for her in Fiesole. Now she wants to go to the opera every night, but in her village there is no opera house. She will even walk a mile to see a solitary cypress tree—they are rare in the misty flatlands of Bedfordshire. I cannot bear to think of my mother for long.

    My girl friend is altogether something else. Back she comes, with three rabbit skins and a broken sewing machine, and she lays them at my feet. She looks up at me, her small face strange between the skins and the machine, but what can I say. I always smile back at her. Then off she goes and takes a long bath, talking to herself. Afterwards, she shakes me violently in the middle of the night, hitting me too, with her fist, and tells me what animals she has seen: "In a dream I have seen other creatures," she says, "I dreamt that an immense plain stretched far behind this house, and looking out on it in the blue morning light I saw all the animals standing quietly, exquisitely, together—lions, great birds and cranes, cows, giraffes, elk and horses and bears and tigers, armadillos, squirrels. Wonderful, so still; all these pure beings in harmony, in that slanting virgin light. I wish you could see them."

    I look around the room and see no animals. I do not even see my girl friend, she is far away now, giving a cooking lesson in Texas. I am deeply perplexed about my room, and so I must stay in it and fight it. No matter which of us wins, the fight will force me to recognize it. It does not belong to me, the room, but to a person who is at present in Buffalo. Is that why my girl friend saw no buffaloes in her dream? That is the kind of displacement I have to fight against. In the middle of the night I get out of bed and walk around the room, seeing no animals. I go for a walk in the streets and I find no rabbit skins, no broken sewing machine. My girl friend is a future, possibly; my room is the present, which I keep trying to escape from. I must stay in here and put my dismantled body together. As it is, my body is in a cupboard in Texas, or somewhere, dismantled, like a weapon someone has wanted to store away.

    Perhaps I can think of my mother again now. Where did she come from? No matter, she is far away. In fact, I am a good bit closer to Italy than she is. This town is full of pizzerias, I can almost hear the pizzas sizzling all around my room. My mother speaks in a curious way, which sometimes, because of her exaggerations and clichés, threatens the balance of my mind. Such a slap-up dinner. Do you want a hotty? Let's have a cuppa. Yet I do believe my mother has soul, which is why she wants to be an Italian. The nocturnal regurgitations might be another kind of displacement: her stomach rejects its contents at night in an attempt to Italianize itself.

My girl friend also dashes across the town and inserts into the mailbox of a person whom we hardly know a message saying: "We miss you terribly." And then hurriedly she scribbles another message, standing by the mailbox, and slips it in. The second message says: "Still." In her dream, the animals too were still. My girl friend has very beautiful knees, dimpled, which would not be as they are if she were not so often on the move. She rushes about with a jangle of saucepans and dinner plates, jumping in and out of a car, or dancing suddenly when the moonlight comes in and wakes her up. We dance together, sometimes, and I would dance with her now, in broad daylight, if she were not giving a cooking lesson or collecting broken chairs and old waistcoats in Texas.

My room is always there when I come back to it, and I am determined to stay in it whenever I come back to it. The present is that which obliges you to identify and decide things; just how difficult that is. . . . One could rage and weep, day and night, rushing from thing to thing in a room, with fists imploring it to reveal itself. What is this it, with which all separate objects conspire? I come in and ask the greyish light in the room: "Are you still? Are you animal?" I change the light by drawing curtains or switching lamps on and off, each change followed by the same questions. By displacing the light I attempt to violate its state of non-identity; and all the time my mother's nocturnal spewings are Italian violations of her native unknown origin.

In my small kitchen there are some dishes which my girl friend touched when she was here.

On a shelf by the bathroom she has left a shirt and a green woollen helmet. How frightening it looked, the waistcoat she brought home one night and left on the balcony in the pouring rain. Like the waistcoat of a bachelor who has just been fished out of the river.

Later she dried it and whisked it away to Texas, a present for her brother. She left me the rabbit skins and a cracked old suitcase, quite small. I have not opened the suitcase yet, for fear of what might be in it. Some animals; or the same empty grey light, which I have not been able to take by surprise.

To my girl friend I write: There was this derelict, an old man, frozen by the roadside. I rubbed his hands for a long time; eventually a little warmth came into them. He kept asking, "Am I still a human being?" I could smell his smell for two days after this. There it was.

To my mother I write about the derelict also, and with a different ending: It took me two days to scrub from my fingers the smell of his mortification.

To this room I say: Here, animal, come sniff my hands.

Ignorance

My visitors are not people; they are not even shadows; it would even be going too far to say that I see them. Yet they are here, in this room, I am certain of it. At least, I am certain at this moment, if that is saying anything.

Once I did see them, or thought so. Several months ago, when I woke up in the night, they were streaming around the walls. Not exactly around the walls, but it was happening, they were here. This was how it began. I looked up from my bed and saw, along the angle where wall and ceiling meet, above the chest of drawers, in the dim light from street lamps, that the visitors were being announced. They must have been leaning against the darkness and the darkness had sprung open. Vague forms, tall somehow, somehow streaming, but even then not quite on my side of the invisible.

Since that night, they have taken up residence, to put it mildly. Everyone who comes into this room, for a moment or so, perhaps an hour or two, notices something. Nothing need be said; yet signs of change can be seen in the faces of people who come to take a drink and shoot the breeze. As for me, I have to put up with them all the time, these visitors.

Not people, not shadows, but here in this room, hovering around the frying pan, the cooking pots, wedged between the pages of books, crouching beneath the rickety table, they breathe at the lamps, touch the flowers, listen to noises from the outside, passing cars, the shouts of children, attentive to the splash of water as the girl moves her arms in the bath. They even warm their hands at the electric oven. They do not say anything, they make no smells, no noises, they have no outlines. I know they are here because I have to live for them, and so does the girl.

Times become more and more strange, for the girl and me. The visitors must have come to know that we are sensitive to them. When there is music, I can't help it, I have to do a dance. I dance naked or in my clothes, day or night, whenever the music takes hold of me. The girl too, up she jumps and she dances, just as often. We also invite lovers, we multiply our lives, because we have to live for the visitors, we have to reckon with them.

Did they never do anything wrong? We shall do it for them, and plenty. Did they always answer letters? We answer none, or, if we do, on occasion, we stick the answers into empty wine bottles. One day they were taken away from this room, they had to leave it, the last whiff of tobacco left their nostrils, long ago, or was it yesterday?

They may not have been dragged away, but they left, packed into grey trucks; each of the visitors carried a small suitcase, containing some clothes, soap, identity papers, a toothbrush perhaps, or a book. The grey trucks roared away down the street, just as the rubbish trucks do now on Tuesday mornings. That was the end of the visitors. They could not come back. If anyone knows where they went, he should declare it. Into some hell hole or other, I have heard many stories. A girl finds a battered old suitcase with nothing in it but a very long white hair; but what has this hair got to do with the stories?

Now the purple prick head swells with their desires, they lick the flesh, lap the froth of love, adrift sobbing among pots and pans, the record player, the lamps, the pictures, and here are bodies dancing for them, or writhing on the bed, in wild embraces. We tell them: Never mind, it doesn't matter. Miserable as they are, nothing we do is too much for them. A well in Spain, a frontier post, a high window, the barrel of a gun between the front teeth, or a cattle truck, searchlights and wire, balls of thumbs hardening as the whips hit—they have had enough of all this. They have come back, in their own peculiar way, nowhere to go but into us, down the shafts they sink through our ribs, or straight into the throat, or piercing the guts by way of the genitals. We shall dance again soon, for breakfast, or when darkness comes, silk and soot, putting a gleam on the leaves of the lime trees outside. We shall scatter and take from this room nothing but the shafts, through which they penetrate us, sunk deep into our flesh, sticking through and out of us, for all the world like porcupines or pomanders, and such it is, this airy tomb the visitors are building around us, it is far, it is here, wing-beat, it is the sperm vivid silver snaking down the girl's back, and it is pain, but it has no wrinkles, only one very long white hair, the sign.

A Memorial to the Room-Collectors

This morning I want to capture for you a quite particular moment. It is the moment at which room-collection shed its early descriptive forms and became something else, a *mysterium*. This may seem irrelevant to us now, as we crouch, stand, or sit in this desert, among these rocks, waiting for the cool of evening to blow across, or watching for sunrise. But you, Ann, you Roberto, you too, Elizabeth, and all of us, we all know that these curiosities of the past help us to endure this time. They help us not to go out of our minds. At any moment they may also serve us as guidelines, if ever our situation should change. So how was it, that moment?

I have mentioned the beginnings of room-collection before, but only in passing. We know that, as earth became overpopulated, the old genius of literature took on a new appearance. Formerly it had been communicated in diverse ways through the book; now it threw all its energies into a vocal task. The room-collectors stood before enormous audiences and described their collections; and the people listening, spellbound, forgot for a while their misery, forgot that they had nowhere to go, forgot that they had, some of them, hardly any space on which to plant their aching feet.

Of these early descriptions we can say that they were crude but convincing. The primitives had, after all, first-hand experience of real rooms. Their recital of measurements, details of décor, furniture, lighting, and other paraphernalia, did have a certain allure. Room-collecting differed from philately, say, or numismatics, to the extent that no specific concrete objects were involved, only descriptions: it was vocal and it was mental. Thus, even in its early phase room-collecting contained the seeds of that more pure, spiritual art which eventually came into being at the moment I wish to capture for you. If you are not comfortable on that rock, Ann, why not try the patch of sand over there? Move over a bit, Sui Sun!

Well now, I have indicated to you what I would like to be able to do, capture that moment. But I am not sure, of course, that I can do so, improvising like this. Even if I could do so, you might not notice that I had done so. That is how it is, the passing moment. A retrospect can frame, somewhat, the flow of time; but this framing brings distortion, which may not really be error, but which certainly can admit falsification of some kind. The great blaze of sense-impressions in which we live looks otherwise than it is or was, as soon as we attempt to freeze it. The most we can look for is some kind of approach to the moment, behaving as if we intended to take it by surprise. Even then, the intent itself may obstruct the unfolding of the true moment, if there ever was or is a moment one can call true, a moment with a coherence having greater magnitude and integrity than the constructions we place upon it.

That ant, Tsëpë, is about to crawl between your toes. Watch it.

I have said that room-collecting was non-possessive. Just think of those primitives of room-collecting. They showed the way to an intimate knowledge of rooms they had actually lived in, seen, or dreamed of. They told of historic rooms, such as the *cabinet de travail* of Catherine de Medici. Of rooms, too, in which they would have liked to live—a low-ceilinged room afloat with subtle light filtered through trees, plane-trees rustling in the piazza on which the room looks out; and another room, on a quiet street in Berlin, eleven paces by nine, with music in it, a high ceiling, and a strange light, as if it were illuminated by an indigo star. They also told of rooms that were stamped on the brains of people who existed only in paintings, or in daguerrotypes: stuffed plush interiors of the Victorian age, children's nurseries alive with toys, even the stink and crush of long-demolished brothels and paddingkens—all these were their materials.

Great social benefits flowed from their descriptions, and as speakers they were much in demand, presenting ample details, anxiously gathered and pleasantly deployed, to audiences with barely a foothold on the earth's surface. They would tell of lordly rooms—large enough to contain a bed and table. Of rooms in ancient palaces, like Chambord and Mycenae, Balmoral and Thebes. They told of the materials used in the construction of such rooms, wood and stone, plaster, brick, mud, adobe, marble, and the rest. More, they showed how these substances came to be impregnated with the presences of persons who had lived in the rooms. The wooden panels, the baked mud walls— imprinted with faces and hair and hands, the atoms of the room-dwellers still there, retained in curtain fabrics and old wallpapers, or in the eye of a painted dolphin, the arc of a swallow's wing. Yet, even at the time when the room-collector's art was beginning to take on a regular and recognizable shape, such actual substances and textures had long since vanished from the consciousness of all but the few who collected and transmitted the original information about rooms.

Do not forget that the task of transmission became more and more difficult, as the words employed to signify this or that detail fell out of use or changed their meanings. There must have been all kinds of misunderstanding. But the collectors went at it; as the years passed, audiences came to feel that they were participating in a rite, only two thirds of which, or less, were intelligible.

The audiences did not only hear, they saw, because now rapidly the art of descriptive transmission developed many nuances and was practised by men and women of great vocal subtlety. They were, these devotees of the art, developing a tradition of which the material origins were already lost. Yet they presented the rooms: prison cells and barrack rooms, rooms in the huts of concentration camps, rooms in which old people lived alone and died alone, rooms too in which schematic luxuries seemed to repulse the inhabitants—imitation wood consoles, plastic chairs, the stereotype gadgets, even a family in residence for years might just as well have been another family. I refer here to rooms in the ancient suburbs of Houston, Paris, Teheran, and so forth. But there were other interiors also, less repulsive ones: Persian nomad tents, Serbian cottage rooms, and cemetery rooms, Egyptian, Etruscan, French *tombeaux*, and old dining rooms not least, public or private—one small makeshift kitchen in which the world's most exquisite cook would prepare meals for her lover, and the pleasing furniture of an *amatorium* in Bacharach. Anecdote: a visitor to the Rothschild *tombeau* in Paris exclaimed—"These people certainly know how to live!" Should we presume, or not, that the visitor was simple-minded?

Eventually specialists came on the scene. Once the initial difficulties had been overcome, there were indeed many specialists. The initial difficulties were: How does one describe a room, anyhow? Does one catalogue its measurements and contents? That method seldom led to higher achievements in the descriptive art. How does one so dispose words in the air as to capture and convey the live atmospheric conditions of a room, the presence it has, its (let us say) psychic proportions? The specialists, backed by the weight and spirit of an evolving tradition, were inevitably a kind of élite. Some, reluctant to appear so, specialized in rest-rooms. One even collected a mass of information about rest-rooms in the old filling stations, such as Gulf or Texaco. Who had been there, what did they find, what did they do? Amazing, when you come to think of it.

Another specialist had a corner in cells, actually not prison cells, but cells in which revolutionaries met to discuss their plans. Prison cells often impinged on this field, it hardly need be said. And yet another specialist compiled a complicated archive for atmospheric analysis of the kinds of interior space once found in hotels. Quite apart from the varieties of physical space involved, what qualities inhered in the transience of the occupants, and did those qualities differ from place to place? What sadnesses, if the travellers were lonesome—what joy and last-moment tearful embraces, if they were lovers.

Not all the special collections were concerned with pleasant rooms. Earlier I mentioned the London paddingkens, or dosshouses, of the Victorian age. The North American flop-house also figured on this score. And those frightful rooms in Victorian paupers' lodging houses, where as many as a dozen people of both sexes occupied a single bug-infested bed, all using the tiny yard outside as a toilet, killing one another or mating with one another as the urge took them. Gruesome details, but they may have brought a thin beam of light into the lives of those people who constituted the trebly miserable audiences of later times. Or those people might have then known an alleviation of their misery, just a slight and tremulous alleviation, when they heard that their sufferings had precedents, and had been shared by earlier dupes of civilization, smashed playthings of a property-based and profit-motivated social system.

I break this gloom with a reference to a poem about an artist's studio. Ann will recite it for us in a moment; it was transmitted to her by Alberto, who, as you know, was taken from us three weeks ago. It is by André Breton, and is called "The Room of Yves Tanguy." Tanguy was a painter; his studio in Connecticut, where he lived for a time in exile, and where he died, mirrored his ascetic and stark imagination. It used to be a collector's item, this poem. Ann? Hang it all, wipe them away with your hand then. All right, we'll have the poem later. There now, hold Caroline's hand.

Onward! Another special field (Breton's poem belongs in a variable context) was the room as depicted in paintings. Vermeer, for instance, painted spacious interiors in which calm people lived, clad in splendidly simple garments, and in which they prepared meals and played musical instruments. In a painting by Vermeer you could see people and things in rooms with good proportions. That part of the room which was hidden, because of the point of view, might appear in a mirror. Or there was a window near one of the portrayed figures. This mirror or window opened up the picture no end. A space was there, containing another space, hidden or reflected. Or the room was an extension of some unconfined and incorporeal reality external to it. Note this. It is important in itself, and it becomes more important as we approach the art of room-collection as a *mysterium*.

We cannot pounce on our moment yet; but, in a preparatory way, remark how a room, an interior enclosed space, may come to function as an analogue of that specific degree of visibility upon which some invisible presence depends for the radiation of its power. That power-radiating presence is not coterminous with the room-collector who is presenting the room, far from it. The room-collector is no more than a snag in the mechanism of pure appearance. Gods and criminals deploy their power in much the same way. They keep out of sight, but there has to be a scene in which their power is manifest to some degree. I shall repeat this formulation, if you like—it's cumbersome, no doubt, but Truett, you needn't look like that.

Back now to the rooms in paintings. There are two interiors by Turner which used to be described. What were they called . . . yes, "A Bedroom in Venice" and . . . "The Music Party, Petworth." The first was a watercolour, the second a body-colour on blue paper. The room in Venice looks as if it is swimming in light: areas of blue indicate a far wall, there is a ridged bed-canopy, bright yellow, and two tall windows occupy the centre and left side of the picture. In the window to the left you could see that very tall tower which stood outside Saint Mark's. The ceiling has a sketchy red design on it, I recall, and some other patches of venetian red dispose a few inklings of furniture in the spacious middle of the room. What a place it must have been, so airy, though damp, perhaps. Much airier than the Petworth room. Here a lady in a long dress is playing a small grand piano, under a low domed ceiling, surrounded by chairs she is, and beyond her some other people in pink and green clothes look as if they have given the music up and are playing cards. Somebody is reclining on a sofa beside the piano-player, suddenly he has raised his head, and the piano-player might be looking at him. Is he telling her to stop? He has brown hair bushing out at the sides, but is bald on the forehead. He has no features. He doesn't look as if he'd care to dance. But the lady at the piano and this man are the soul of the party.

One important controversy arose between specialists over the question of two types of space: secular and sacred. This sort of question has often perplexed and enraged people. A sacred space is one that is firmly marked off from its surroundings. It is set aside. The surprising thing was that the question should have been posed at all during the epoch of demographic catastrophe. Perhaps the troubles of that time stirred up old sedimentary problems. The controversy came about like this: at a gathering in Epidavros, itself a sacred space, a renowned room-collector was quietly addressing the multitude on a rare topic, the old pilgrimage cathedral at Vézelay, when suddenly he was shouted down by a frantic colleague. This colleague insisted that sacred space was not the domain of room-collectors at all. His argument was commonplace, so that even a fair section of the public understood. He said that a room had to have, or to be there for, an occupant, however temporary that occupant might be; and that a sacred space had no occupant, strictly speaking, at best it might enshrine a purely potential presence. This stopped the speaker, there were terrible cries from the frustrated public, and a hurried consultation ensued (the occasion was a festival of room-collecting and many specialists were present). It was decided that a debate should be held that night *in camera*. Meanwhile the next speaker came on. His special field was the *cabinet de travail* of Catherine de Medici at Blois. He pacified the audience, with an account of its two hundred and thirty-seven small wooden panels, each different, its two doors, and its secret closet, which you could open by pressing your foot on a hidden spring near the floor. A pleasant room, by all accounts, as long as the poisons and death-sentences remained safely in the closet.

Now listen carefully. We may be beginning our approach. Is it all right now, Ann? How does that piece of dried rabbit taste, Harold? Give me a bit of space can you, folks, I have to concentrate.

One thing we do know is that a description of a room turns out to be a blank if all you describe is the ensemble of that room's physical properties. None of you can remember a room, right? But they were spaces enclosed by materials of some kind, that much you do know, and you also know that you had to go in and out (doors), as well as looking out and in (windows). These enclosed spaces had hundreds of different functions: eating, sleeping, dancing, drinking, reading, being punished, peeing, being cut open, being questioned, dying, and so forth. Hundreds of different functions, which were only on occasion interchangeable. So it was, at least as regards the room as traditionally recognized long before our time. Now a description of such a space is an enterprise undertaken with a view to capturing some unbidden, but slowly emerging, gradually noticeable presence which is quite special to the room in question. Do we have to eliminate airports? Aren't they transit areas without any presence at all? One of the early primitives (Perec, from Brittany) used to tell of a friend who had lived for a month in an airport, to try it out, but that case was exceptional. And yet what about Czechoslovak castle chapels taken over by interrogators and police archivists? What identity can be attributed to a room with a twisted function? As the art of description evolved, several kinds of rooms with twisted functions came to figure in the descriptions. However, the room as visible and somehow integral function of a presence remained the real issue. Not necessarily the presence of actual occupants. Not necessarily ghosts. But a presence of some kind. A *living* space, really dwelt in, that was the issue. Very different, substantially so, from a schematic or dead space.

Of that nocturnal debate among specialists in Epidavros we know nothing. My hunch is that a certain unusual type of room-collecting was forced underground at that point. The orthodox collectors were prepared to admit the reality of the presence, as a key factor in room-description. But there was a limit beyond which they would not go. Others, possibly beset by dangers and yielding to correction, faded out. Others again, a handful, may have hankered after a vision of what lay outside the limit; these may even have developed ways to encode that hankering, inconspicuously, in their vocal presentations, whenever the coast was clear. But there were some, very few, who could not accept the limit as anything but a conceptual convenience. These were the room-collectors who raised the descriptive art to the status of a spiritual art—of which now hardly a trace remains. These room-collectors were intent on tracing, with extreme subtlety and acute powers of perception, the minute shifting differences, or ligaments, between secular rooms and sacred spaces.

Here is an example, transmitted to me two years ago, by a very old man whose name I have clean forgotten. We were wedged, that day, between two ferocious throngs of white men who were throwing dice (actually bones) for a tiny patch of ground on which someone wanted to have a baby. Odd as it seems, I could hear distinctly every word the old man spoke. He must have been a room-collector, in his time. He told me of a painting by Giovanni Bellini (ah, Giovanni, so you lift up your head, now listen). The painting shows a saint in a brown monk's robe, in a rocky landscape, with a cheerful donkey in the middle ground, and in the background a town with walls and towers. On a hilltop, a palace, or fortress. Above that, a deep blue sky with clouds curling across it. To the left of the foreground stands a curving tree, tall, bushy at the top. Planted there on his platform of rock, the saint tilts his upper body back, and his hands are turned palms outward, the arms almost at full stretch and raised a little from his sides. His head also tilts back. As if he were imitating the tree. Or as if a wave of force had hit him in the chest. But behind him, on the right-hand side of the picture, is a dark cave, its opening faces you. Outside the opening, a rough structure transforms three slender trees into an arbour, with a bench—it is a plain board attached to the lower parts of the tree trunks. A reading desk, with a sloping top and well-carpentered uprights, held firm by crossbars on two levels, is placed so that you can sit on the bench with your back to the world and read scripture. A skull is placed on the horizontal board that leads off from the sloping desk-top; and a delicate osier trellis divides this open-air study from the dark mouth of the cave.

There you have it. Definitely a room makes its appearance here. The details signify precisely those differences and ligaments between contrary kinds of space. But notice how transparent everything, differences included, has become. The saint can stand there, barefoot, with his palms and his eyes turned to the world, which he receives full in the body, and which he blesses (cheerful donkey). Or the saint can sit there, with a jug for drinking vessel always in reach of his left hand, while he contemplates the scriptures or gazes across the skull into the dark interior of the cave.

It is a picture, if you like, in which a presence, that of the saint, embodies the single root of unconscious and conscious life, while neither the picture nor this interpretation deny the reality of phases in between, differences, ligaments. Remember that strange saying: "What were the firefly's light, if it were not for darkness? The one implies the other." Who said that? We no longer know. But we feel for the Latin way in which he released the full sensory character of the word "implies." The saying itself is a room worth collecting.

What the old man told me collided in my mind with something I had been told long before that woeful game of dice. This: I mentioned Vézelay and now here is a sketch of what you might have seen and felt there, if you had ever been a pilgrim those many hundreds of years back in time. Entering this building you would have seen before you an enormous space, like a barrel or a gigantic womb. To go in there you would pass through a great door, over which, describing a semicircle, was the so-called tympanum (if that is the word). In the middle of the semicircle stood a figure in stone, some sort of god, and around him in an arc were arranged the heavenly signs, Ram, Bull, and the rest. Then, even further out from the central figure, arched yet another band of figures showing everyday activities of that time, such as ploughing and reaping. The god stood, upright and physical, in the centre of all this whirling time, for the bull and the ram and the ploughman were all crystallizations of time.

Now you penetrate the enormous space, crawling on your knees perhaps, there is plenty of noise, chanting and muttering, many other pilgrims all around you, and all sorts of smells attack your nostrils, incense and sweat, stale fruit, cloves, the smell of feet. Eventually you reach the surface sanctuary, but already someone is tugging your elbow and you turn left, down a flight of stone steps, into a crepuscular subterranean place, lit only by a few candles.

The floor is uneven, solid rock made slippery by the tread of many feet, bare, in rags, or booted. The veins in the rock stand out, as if it had been petrified in the midst of a tremendous muscular effort; or it looks like a frozen sea. All of a sudden before you is the shrine which contains some oddments, bones and stuff, which, so you believe, for you have been told it is so, once belonged to a woman who actually washed the god's feet and dried them with her glorious hair. After all this, and after the weeks of footslogging, you felt more than just removed from family, friends, the working everyday life. You felt rapt away from ordinariness altogether. You were in the presence of something constant, but terribly fugitive, not merely something potential, but actual. You felt fright, joy, pain, and these were painfully clear feelings. Briefly, you had arrived at a centre of time and a centre of space.

The magic of presence is what you felt, and this feeling was yours because you had slipped away from ordinary existence. You had found the deviation which leads who knows where. Now in your bones you knew something else, other than existence made of edges, leftovers, limits where the wheel's rough rim grinds everything to powder. You were still in a crowd, of course, but this feeling made you, for as long as it lasted, somebody special. In that presence, you were free to be everything the living universe had planted in your flesh and in your mind. At that moment, you broke into flower.

Of course, some falsification came into this. Pilgrimages to Vézelay became no more than a trickle when an alternative set of sacred bones turned up further south. And many hundreds of years after that, when travel became a secular sort of pilgrimage, tourists would sometimes feel not illuminated but deceived. The illusion, as somebody once said, of having vanquished distance and obliterated time, of being far out—that illusion could be fraught with pain. Or else we might say that beliefs imply fictions which may rest upon what some of us would call falsifications, although much depends on how you view the visible world, as something solid, or as volatile energy frisking about in the air.

Have we overshot the moment, on our travels? No. It was this rediscovery of the experience of flowering that transformed the room-collector's art into a spiritual art, surpassing description, evocation, conjuring tricks and the rest. Certainly the art went underground at that point. It had found new tasks. Now I see Russell scratching a hole in the dirt with his fingernail, Elizabeth too! Have I been too charming? Scratch on, we are here to scratch; but be sure to couple it with thinking. Now we can listen to the poem, it is not a long one.

Nine Biplanes

for Ricardo Gullón

una vaga astronomía
de pistolas inconcretas
   —Federico García Lorca

Summer 1940: I opened the double glass front door of that rambling country mansion, school, and saw nine biplanes flying low, in close formation, and slowly; the lower edge of what I saw is a ruffled green mass of trees.

But I do not know what day it was, or the month, only that the summer had begun. And there may have been six biplanes, or twelve. Certainly they were biplanes, heavy ones, with two motors, and they were moving slowly, as if a great wind belaboured them, though the trees were hardly moving, there was no wind, or just a little. I opened the front door, was standing on the gravel path which looped a large flower bed, and then came the noise.

Now, looking out of the window, I see a low wall of rocks, a section of grey drainpipe stood on end as the base for a bird feeder, a green bush, and behind these, somewhat higher, a mass of foliage, and behind the foliage a sky, frameless, though parcelled into infinity by bird calls delineating territories, and beyond that, the real sky. A child looking the same way sees deep down, a window, and deeper, little pine tree, clear lake, another window, and deeper, little pine tree, its image, in a clear lake.

The noise is still loud and clear. Looking upward I saw the biplanes. I had heard about the war, but nobody had said much about it, except, now, that the Germans had broken through. They said it, yet one saw nothing; at any moment, they said, it might happen, the invasion. They, whoever they were, spoke of invasion, invasion, and there we were, eating toast, miles from home, running up and down the long corridors, and doing extra Latin. The schoolmaster went on smoking his pipe, whacking us with his slipper, and writing neat equations with his goldnibbed Onoto pen. It was an odd thing, so much noise, overhead, and rushing out of the house, more than a house, a country mansion, after crossing the immense panelled hall, and opening the door, and now to be standing there on the gravel, looking up, and seeing the biplanes.

Nine or six biplanes, already oldfashioned, as one knew from pictures in the papers, flying somewhere, to fight, in the sky, somehow, the Germans, who had broken through.

Deeper still, a street in Hué or An Loc, no, this time Barcelona, and a little girl's head being sliced off by a bomb splinter, her mother clutching at the body, two soldiers in bedraggled uniforms looking at the head, down at the head, which lay at their feet.

They were flying across Norfolk, toward the sea perhaps. Woods, the breckland, miles of wheatfields and dark barns, heading toward the sea. The Germans were not at sea at all. What were they looking for? How would they identify it when they found it? They had been told to fly. So they flew, airmen, wearing leather helmets, which are not blown off their heads because of the leather straps and the buckles. Signals from their home base filling the cockpits, determined looks on their goggled faces, the air humming among the wires we drew crisscross between the two wings when we made our sketches.

When people are blocking the French road, exploding steel mouths gobble their canaries, grandparents, and bolsters. Deep down, a clear lake, it reflects the sign to be seen in a certain Moscow elevator in 1937: It is prohibited to put books down the lavatory.

They sat in the cockpits, looking determined, with orders to fight the Germans, if they found them, knowing that their machines were rickety and ridiculous. Maximum speed 150 m.p.h. Down there on the gravel I heard the droning clatter of their motors. Type of armament: unknown. Range: uncertain.

Seeing German soldiers marching into the Saarland, they were marching on the front page of the *Daily Sketch*, made me ask one day in the basement kitchen, with the paper spread out before me on the kitchen table among jampots and knives and cups: So is there going to be a war? My mother at the stove, without turning around to face me, must have said Yes or No, probably No; but with the biplanes flying in close formation low overhead, I was not remembering this.

The men wearing helmets and sitting in the cockpits of the old biplanes were not twiddling their thumbs or drinking pop, but they were English. Perhaps they knew about the bombing in Spain, whereas I knew nothing, or had noticed nothing, except the Crystal Palace Fire, the Abdication, the faraway deep throbbing at sea through late summer nights, before September, when German armies marched into Poland, and Polish cavalry with sabres launched attacks on tanks, I knew nothing about bombing in Spain but thought I must have heard fleets of submarines moving out into the Atlantic. So these airmen were setting out, on a summer's day in the fifteenth century, to fight the enemy, flying low, in close formation, and I had rushed through the panelled hall, had opened the door, and now stood and stared at them, my feet on the gravel, my head tilted back, mouth open, and did not realize that this was what was happening. A loud noise in the sky, continuous. Antique gesture.

A child, instead of looking downward, now looks outward, and still cannot awake, the inability to awake being, like an arm's reach or the tilting of a head, part of his condition. With hacked-off hands he constructs for himself someone else, old, scribbling. Amid the droning clatter of the motors, a bell of pink fire suddenly sounds. He listens to the long trumpet blaring tightly across the neolithic heath, on which he found flints during Sunday afternoons; he listens to the flying metal blare and does not see the girl's head rolling across the gravel to his toecaps.

The sounds are people running in plimsolls, knock of the red leather ball on the willow cricket bat. A smell of linseed oil in the thatched pavilion. But the pilot's head is wrapped in leather: the pilots are going to knock the Germans for six, if they can find them, behind the pavilion, between the pavilion and the woods, where you could hear the cock pheasant scream before any thunderstorm, or, in the evening twilight, quietly see rabbits feeding, their ears laid back along their little skulls.

ent of
2

Or Else

As I went into the tabac to buy two boxes of matches, I happened to glance to my right. Or else, as I glanced to the right on going into the tabac to buy two boxes of matches, or else I had gone into a tabac to buy two boxes of matches, and glancing to the right I saw a small woman, not old, not young, perched on a chair, and she was eating what I took to be a tartine, or else the remnant of a tartine. She held the bread in both hands, like a squirrel, and her feet did not touch the floor. She was a very small person, and her face was round and white.

Then I asked for the matches, paid for them, and while turning to leave took a second look at the small woman. It was a small tabac, too, with only two or three tables and chairs lined up against the wall, and a mirror ran along the wall, reaching to the floor. The woman, perched on the chair, her feet not touching the floor, was half-turned toward the wall, she took a bite at her tartine, leaving behind a white streak of bread in her two clasped hands.

She sat turned away from the rest of the tabac. But she was so small that her round white face hardly appeared in the mirror. She ate like a trapped animal. She did not want to be seen. She did not want to see herself, yet, turning her face away from the space of the tabac, she almost had to be seeing herself, in the mirror, and also in the mirror the inescapable tabac space in which she felt conspicuous.

Or else: she was a very small woman with a round white face which nobody wanted to see, not even herself, but she had to be somewhere, in order to eat. Still, she was eating in such a way as to indicate that she wanted to live, hands clasping bread, even if living meant disappearing.

All around her, all around me, in that small space, the packets of cigarettes and the boxes of matches, the people walking in the street, on their way from the day's work, in their appropriate clothes, and the dogs going about their business, and the continuous roar of all the cars.

Or else: I cannot say all around us. No link. No common root, at best a rhizome, contrived by the other bodies and the noises, in their scatteredness, connected her particularity and mine, within a surface of observation more fleeting even than the last white shred of her tartine at which I saw her now sucking, not chewing, no, but sucking.

The question of her teeth had not yet arisen. Strong teeth, squirrel teeth, grow in straight jaws, but hers might be weak teeth, in such round jaws. She lacked the courage, or else the presumption, to use a good toothpaste, and this had been going on for years. Nor had she the means to visit a dentist. Or else she had once scraped and saved, had once made an appointment, but the dentist had sent her away the moment he saw her. A tartine has a strong crust. So many sacrifices, in such a life. The cheapest food, a tartine, with ham or jam, and a little butter. Even then, she had to eat the tartine in her particular way, by sucking, and in public, she had to turn her face aside and not look, she wanted to eat while being invisible, she had a passion of great force, dangerous, for the tartines of this tabac, and here the rhizome put forth another bud, because in her I saw another being who had to aim, straight-on, for the impossible.

Or else: I went into the tabac after spending an afternoon with a young woman, small and beautiful, with a laugh like the silver trickle of starlight seen in the water of a well. We had walked across bridges and along corridors, we had exchanged sweat from the palms of our hands, we had sat beside one another with mirrors behind us, gazing out into the world, or gazing at each other, in the envious ancient way of Assyrians; but who, now, among the ancient Assyrians would care to wonder about the small woman with the round white face, or who else, one century or two from now, in Paris, would want to know that she existed?

She might never have been touched. I saw her short legs, white and lumpy, because, the way she sat, twisting away from the world, her skirt was hitched up to her knees. Nobody had ever wanted to stroke them. With her weak teeth she had never bitten anybody. With her small and frightened mouth she had never sucked anybody. Or else nobody living one century or two from now, no ancient Assyrian either, would, unless I am mistaken, want or have wanted to be bitten, or else sucked, by the small woman with the round white face and the unstroked legs.

She was not a tiny soldier in the battle against chance, so by chance she had to be a nullity. When she looked in a mirror and saw herself, she might have found it hard to believe that this was all she was: not even worth a glance, but worse—a pretext for averting every glance. Round, small, white zero, with a circumference nobody would dream of stroking into place, thus not even, really, a zero. The continuous roar of traffic. The dogs going about their business. Perched on the chair, a blob of absolute anxiety. Blob—and there they go, the beautiful ancient Assyrians, and others, who can be seen, who think it is they who happen, not chance, who receive existence from a knowledge that they are to be seen; and there they go, the dogs, capering and sniffing, a blob in their track is a small woman with a round white face and wet-looking hair which nobody wants to comb or pat; a blob sucking a tartine in a tabac and looking aside, or else down, she wants only not to be there where everyone else happens to be going.

Or else I am mistaken, entirely mistaken, and what I see is a large and very beautiful flea. A star among the fleas. And the dogs, in holy terror, worship her? From flea to angel, the spectrum of perception bends and cracks under the buffetings of chance, as, in a changed perspective, a world of different objects comes into position. Lens-grinding Spinoza says to the small woman (she does not hear, and I may not have heard correctly): "Every being which is made conscious of its interior power comes to persevere the more insistently in its particular nature."

Never once did anything occur to the small woman such as might have shown her that plenitude of interior power. She perseveres because she has been doomed to do so, by the dogs in the street, or else like them, by the space of the tabac, by the mirror which has finally annulled even her capacity to despair of herself. Or else: A chair in a small tabac, her twisted body insisting on it, is this a likely perch for the Celestial Globe-Hopper, the Pure Flea Spirit? Passing from Spinoza's triangle to the cube, I put one box of matches in my coat pocket, the other in my trouser pocket, and could not say whether or not I was mistaken. Or else I had ground this lens not cruelly enough, for I felt mounting in my throat a galaxy of tears; or else I was grinding into the lens not this indelible presence but my own shadow, nicotine, idiotic.

Louise Moillon's Apricots (1635)

She has allowed the absolute standpoint of a twenty-year-old woman to be consumed by a heap of apricots in a long basket. The apricots in their basket are on a table, the front edge of which is paler than its remoter edge; and here on the front edge there are drops of water, five of them, at one of which a fly is sipping. The spectacularly detailed little fly is wearing wings of a delicately veined fabric.

The other drops of water, various in size, are in that perfect condition which precedes eruption or evaporation. They, in their way, though transparent, are as radiantly corporeal as the apricots.

To the left of the group of four drops of water there is an apricot that has been sliced open; the kernel is still attached to its hollow in the one half. To the right of the fly's drop, there are two apricots, whole, and across them a leafed twig is placed, while attached to the flyward end of the twig are two dark purple shining fruits, probably plums.

Every visible apricot has a bloom, but only on a few is this bloom so noticeable as to be almost an aura. The basket which contains the apricots is made of dark, aged reeds. The apricots stand, or rather they configure, against a background which is black, opaque, impenetrable. Is it really a heap of apricots? Their golden and rotund volumes are casually consorted; it is not so much a heap as an ordering of apricots. Some are resting, each one at its own tilt or angle, on others which are lodged in the middle of the heap, and still others can be seen as a third and remoter group, closer to the darkness. The tripling of the picture space, darkness upward and behind, golden rounds in the middle, and in the foreground the pale brown table surface and edge, is apparent also in this terracing of the apricots.

It is thinkable that she ordered the apricots in this fluid recessive way, each apricot with its twin rondures meeting in the tender sweep of its crease, even though not many display this crease, so as to discourage any donjuanesque counting of the apricots; but also in anticipation that someone, sooner or later, would be certain to count them, someone would ascertain that there are twenty-nine apricots in the basket, and that the number twenty-nine is one of those that are not divisible without a rupture of number into fractions.

There are, however, eight apricots that are so placed as to show the crease, nine, if the apricot on the far right, outside the basket, and on the surface of the table, is included. Also the apricot farthest to the left, but only second highest in the heap, diagonally across from the other, has a crease that is set at a contrastive angle to that of the lower right-hand apricot. The two halves of a circumflex accent, drawn apart, anchor thus each extremity of the left-to-right diagonal from heap to table. It is thinkable that she put her own cocked eyebrow, interrogatively, into the picture.

What is more, the fluid recessive triple-terraced heap of twenty-nine apricots rests in a lining, or nest, of leaves. This nest is hardly noticed at first. Each leaf has sharp, staggered points, six or more. The group of leaves across the top of the heap is not so fresh; no crisp points. These leaves, against the opaque dark background, look wilted, they are contaminated, perhaps by the darkness: one of them is only half a leaf, the absent half has been eaten away, and another has a distinct black hole in it.

Apart from a subjection of certain leaves to an alien and tainting mouth, what can be felt? The spikiness of the leaves around the apricots warns any mouth that all is not so sweet and velvety as one might suppose; as one might suppose, on seeing with one's mouth, even before the eyes have come to the matter, that the seductively edible, creased and golden fruits are for all the world like virgin quims, waiting to enjoy and to be enjoyed. She is saying: Don't you be so sure, these curves are analogues of us, curved ribs, which even our creator could or would not lean upon to make straight. But as a woman she was saying also to women: In you, bodies, there is the presence, a treasure; too soon a leaf goes limp, too late the spikes bristle against the intrusive prick, the eyeballs—

Because the subject is so familiar, you might hang this picture in your kitchen for a year or two and never notice, never really care. The one care might be for the drops of water and the fly. She spent more time lavishing her skill and attention on them, than could ever have been encompassed by any actual co-existence of theirs on the forward edge of the table. Here, too, the accent of her eyebrow, putting a question. Or the diagram of a prolonged insight, a frenzy transfixing an instant, makes the presence violently manifest, as wonder. No, that cannot be it, that cannot be exactly it. A noun phrase or two cannot reflexively represent what she perceived and created as a complex hypotactical sentence, dominated by an as yet uninvented verb-series.

Green and gold, spiked leaf and vulnerable *mons*, the tainting dark and the dance of apricots across the kitchen, forgotten, explored, what happened, Louise, you were a Protestant, in the Cevennes I have seen the museum of the desert where the atrocities inflicted upon your people are commemorated. Actually your eyebrows circumflexed a mystery which we have still not chattered away: Is the presence real, do intervening mediations obliterate it, have we not yet invented any language for it? Is nothing immediate? When it happens, now, and someone coming into the kitchen suddenly winces at the shock of a new cell originating in his brain, that sharp shock, is it paintless and nameless? Or is it graduable into ontological regions, subtle removes, the provinces of difference?

Bless you, do not see wounds as apricots inflicted on the darkness, no, I meant to put it the other way. Place yourself otherwise; be vigilant, but without anxiety, which means—do not interfere with it, let your folds unfold to envelop that force, though it is terrible, mind your reed basket is ventilated and does not dry out. The basket exists for the ordering of apricots, it is the cage of ribs in which each one of them contends for its time, the apricots, which are not weightless, they press against one another, and only the drops of water, really, fly up, evaporating. The fly, the fly is a heavy being, a twinge in the bruise. Of that bruise the two plums are telling, also otherwise, soothed by the twig that is laid horizontally across them, a touch. But look: where the twig was torn off, a flitch of white shows, another wound, the lowest factor, in the right-hand corner, a little curl of white, or a snarl, ridiculously completing all the curves of all the apricots.

Again, begin to read the apricots. Because the deeper tones of gold are among those on the right, and these tones are in an ironic concord with the darkness of the ground, you will respond to a compulsion to reverse the mechanics of any European text—and see from right to left. The creases in the apricots obligingly shift their angles that way also, relatively clockwise. Yet, having made this reversal, you wonder why you made it, why you did not read from the relatively stronger illumination of the apricots on the left, why you did not swivel your eyes then slowly to the right, following an anti-clockwise jerking of the creases toward the deeper tones, unbinding the spell of time.

Precisely that act of wonder suspends any absolute viewpoint—with nothing lost to indeterminacy. This is the threshold across which Keats listened to the nightingale, and on which he constructed, for wonder, a Grecian urn, which also had three groups of figures, deities, or mortals, or both, in frozen ecstasy around it. Louise put her fly on that threshold, in relation to the absolutes of levity—the tight-skinned drops of water; and to the collapsible, heavy, fugitive fly corresponds, in other mythologies, the prince of all metamorphosis, the frog.

Her liminal fly, her to-be-absolute water-drops, her present apricots, and this great bruising darkness—all the visible, little, fugitive bodies enact in a configuration the magic of an oneiric etymology. "Abri"—shelter, dark shield, death a refuge, at least, and "cot"—a more minuscule non-lexical non-seme could hardly exist. There could be no lighter consonant, no rounder vowel, than in the sound of "co[t]." It has no gravity of signification at all. Yet that non-word's oneiric axis generates a small whirl of shadowy relatives: Rabelaisians might find that it verges toward a word now lost, "cotal," meaning penis; "coter" is what surveyors and engineers have to do, measuring land for buildings, plotting a site for a construction; and "cotir"—sometimes for rustics, even if this one did not know it until this very instant when he looked it up—means "to bruise," as a fruit is bruised.

From *Serpentine*

Ingestion   Repast   Transgression
—a Sumerian tablet and other legacies—

The tablet being divided into an upper and lower segment by a deeply incised horizontal line: in the upper segment four adjacent oblong subdivisions contain from left to right two different but vegetal forms and then a hill or eggcup with another tree like a fishbone and then a chocolate grinder or coffeepot (copper à la turque) with a billhook and in the fourth the palm of a left or the back of a right hand. In the lower segment planted at equal intervals across an open space a five-pronged short-handled fork or candlestick and yet another fishbone tree and lastly but now enlarged the first of the two diagonally opposite vegetal forms which might also be a human form erect beside an altar upon which is balanced a sacrificial pot

In the first three upper oblongs just under the lip of the tablet are deep dents like toothmarks

A shopping list or a bill of lading or else

Who groped for this cookie and bit it with dogteeth to break open new ground in consciousness Who took it when it was still soft and etched in the clay these telltale ciphers Who so read an experience as to make of it seven distinct glyphs but left not a shadow of syntax for the sun to inculcate

Sun glare on a bronze breast plate and anterior to it the heart beat of human Agamemnon

Children roasted in a sealed clay pot point fingerbones at Iphigenia

She walks through the curtains of night that are held back by the moon's nacreous hook

She walks to the altar over which she will be thrown to have her throat cut like a goat while a worker family in Berlin 1883 has a meal by the window with the placidity of everyday

To go back to the evil done by Atreus to evil Thyestes—but in what time back of beyond did this Atridean stain start and what covenant was broken at that past repast opening rifts between natural and cultural segments of the norm as in the pot the flesh of children fell from their bones and fallen from the tree the fruit rotted

—Tell us if you are there Artemis protectress of the young and wild creatures

—Tell us Artemis who taking pity on the pregnant hare and abominating the banquet of the eagles headed for Troy in beaked and creaking ships thrusts into Agamemnon's throat the mutinous bone on which he might choke

Nervous laugh of a woman who has wept much

"My stupid room" (in Berlin 1883)—"facing me Dell'Era's eternal smile—Valhalla—Cascabel manqué—melancholy of the human serpent..."

From the Syrian desert in 374 *"serpenti terram comedenti adhuc cibo sumus* still I am food for the serpent which by God's decree devours the earth"

A stone drops into the pool and is in effect while sinking still perceptible in the rings around which are ranged as its limiting recipient natures the feasters with lifted forks and trees weighted with fruit upon the dark earth bearing wheat and barley the ewes drop young without stint as Homer chanted the sea grants fish and the people flourish for good rule and straight judgement issue from the hand of a godfearing king

And the pool cannot be re-entered nor can that stone be retrieved nor of the dent of its weight made among other stones on the floor of the pool can any trace be found let alone scooped up with fork or finger to be set by the candlestick upon the table of sacrifice as a gift offering

Or else at her father's table Iphigenia still could sing the chant that made good the libation and crisped into lawful accord the misty feelings of all but the ancestors who feasted

This Is Lavender

This is lavender and how it grows large blue caterpillars run parallel up their slopes and down in convex furrows never stop following contours a whole field of ripples flows in large blue caterpillars lavender caterpillars large and blue running and flowing up and down and whole blue adjoining fields are solid blue until you move and then the whole solid blue lavender field swishes open like a fan

Easy to stoop run thumb fore and middle finger up a stalk and pluck off the head it is a cluster of little pellets they are the lightest things to touch imagine crushed in your palm an oil in them releases a perfume large and blue ripples up the bone and gristle nose cavities swishing over diminutive salty skin pits in which hairs took root and seesaws along membranous ducts flowing straight into the brain

Brings back to it from far beyond the memory of the sea and next the sea itself they say the brain started in the waves in parallels furrowed never stopping followed the pull of the moon so you hope you are coming close and closer to being in there and flowing in the blue caterpillar parallels or those identical caterpillars flowing over the ripples might come close and closer to being in your seaborn brain which is only a way of saying how the lines consist of letterpellets and out of the rippling caterpillar field

A text develops or does not develop only an analogy the lavender is always out there and if you propose to yourself to go into it or be engulfed in it never to come out again lapsed into a foretime on the slopes of the whitebacked mountain remember that the wish is not the half of it for what you really want is to go into the lavender only as an eye goes through a lens a magnifying lens through it you descry

Large blue being as it flows in vast blue undulations or little ripples letterpellet shaped very far indeed from average distracted jackhammer chatter storytelling hunger poverty and pain the quote nations and classes locked in historic struggle unquote yes large blue being is what you wish to go into inhaling the lavender perfume and crushing the little pellets in your palm with a finger you are wondering

What is this place where there is so much illusion of the holy as if it were a crossingpoint where it begins for it cannot begin nowhere and this is next to nowhere as nothing flows nothing runs it is just the wind if caterpillars ripple pathetic fool you had forgotten that a little further along the slopes of the whitebacked mountain are silos for nuclear

Warheads immense cavities scooped out of the limestone membrane ready to go at the touch of a button and these blue caterpillars ring a peculiar oblong compound where nobody is allowed to stop never stop says the pancarte and they mean it just you keep going

The Green Heron

The green heron stood leaning forward against air currents, although no wind was blowing. Leaning forward, also not like the winged statue clad uniquely in her fan of innumerable folds, but more in promise than in posture—less torpedo than immense tadpole, and entirely singular. He stood with his body leaning forward parallel to the bough of the oak, quilted grey wings held snug to his sides, the maroon neck extended, the elongated triangle of his beak, pointed and black, probing air currents.

The golden iris of his eye, round as a coat button, what might have been reflected in it? How could it stay so wide open, this eye, without blinking? What ghostly marshes, phantom rivers, what nests of stick, what eggs were to be remembered and foreseen by it? A memory for once undisfigured, accurate as starlight, but not shaped like any sort of vessel; a memory that radiated, without strain, stretch, or bend, as action, always to the given limit. His call, a murmur that first rattled in his throat and quickly became, as the long pointed beak opened, an arched but single sound, yeowk, half question, half protest.

Slow wingbeats and fast flight, toward water, or low across water. Exact placing of sounds around him, and always time enough for the appropriate reaction. He listened for the sounds as he answered the touch of air currents. A world of pressures, unmistakeable signs of pressures approaching, desisting, his wings quilted, as if modelled by the imprints of such pressures: a creation of the air, leaning forward into it, opening with his body a bay in the soft front it now offered, conniving with it, resisting its adverse accidents, breathing its luminosity into a darkness interior to his compulsion to breathe it out into itself;

and so, back again, the air, hidden, molding the bow of his breast, the quilting of his wings, reciprocates the mystery of his interior darkness, and beauty, his or otherwise, relates to that which resists, in the instant, or slow in its flight across the centuries, any onset of disfigurement, and to that which does not yield, but still receives, it lends a golden eye so blank it cannot even represent to itself any powers of darkness.

Commodus

Being provisionally unemployed I feel through all the hurt to my dignity more than ever in touch with the plebs perhaps for all my ghostly condition a solidarity with their—

What can I say since always it was the object of my outrages and hence remains entirely vague— flesh? bellybuttons and blades of shoulders stuck out when the axe blade is plucked from a cleft in a log or armour clapping shut over biceps or greaves that close over pitiful thin shins   flexed knees of cobblers fingers of smiths

The last carnal words I heard them say: *unco trahatur unco trahatur* in the senate soon after they had chanted with the selfsame cadence to my glory other words the bastards I never could credit their stuffed nostrils and stuffing paroles with any least perception of the real whiff I got when I stood cheek by jowl in changing rooms with gladiators or when a wicked twitching cunt breathed (*semper infidelis*) into my face

In bedclothes they wrapped me and bounced me away marked surplus equipment in an inconspicuous cart to be dumped in a villa for a time and quickly buried after being identified

My last act was to oil with my vomit the hands of Narcissus (such a pal) who strangled me in the bedclothes I liked it and remembered the dream my mother had had to whisper of

Twelve years they would say and how about it when will you grow up? Twelve years and as many if not more conspiracies

Now an emperor you will understand is not an ostrich

Eventually ostriches arrived and with arrows I shot them in the burning arena with arrows tipped with small bronze crescents

    Saw flies buzz at the array of javelinned lions   Saw the looks on faces crookedly aghast when before them I hoisted a hacked off ostrich head and wagged my own and grinned

Only wanted to tell them better to perish as a lion than as an ostrich (there were no lions for I had invented metaphor to turn them all into ostriches)

Like the buffoons and concubines whose timing was perfect I had put carnival into everything and for all time

Like the statues of myself that hung around looking vacant but more glazed than me my timing was hideously perfect

So I was loved by the plebs and abominated by the ostriches

In the manner of Domitian I penned a death list and left it on a couch where with my playmate I took a nap but that naked boy picks it up to play with

Snakes in his hair   Wings on his back   A little golden bush   A toy!   He runs to Marcia

Hitherto shrieking commands among my cooks and my concubines she is dumbstruck: Her name is first on the list
He stands there panting and scratching his groin Another plot finally thickens

O the raw power of divinity! Red meat of being a god! The bleeding beef the sweet breads of Hercules! But to my opponents

I permitted only blunt swords mine being honed sharper than the razors I declined to use

I singed my own beard and golden curly hair and I spoke with a barbarian accent

Poor papa   Ulcerous philosopher   Anxious always about borders to be patrolled and defended in horror of the Pannonians or the Moesians   I went for the centre but always I hit the uttermost edge (I was left-handed)

A toy empire with toy people and my toy body reeking in the middle of it

Conspiracies cooked up by Cleander and earlier by the buggerish Saoterus upon whose lips I fixed kisses when Rome rushed out to reach me and an event was staged to placate my furious young divinity with chariots and speed limits

Conspiracies: Cleander stockpiled the corn supply to hike prices and he sold senatorial offices   What a vulgar greedy Greek that one was   To his credit they will say he used me but not to mine for he never made anything but use of anyone   I even missed the old thrill when they lopped his head off   A tip: never appoint a proconsul without first detaining his kiddies then off he crawls to Marsilia Lugdunum or wherever and those kiddies kick up their heels back home as pervertible hostages   Terrify everybody

O Hercules hero against evil you were my paragon

As for authority make a display to coerce chance into suiting yourself   *Fortuna semper in vultum pedit* but if you lose as a man you might win as a god   Hottest displays incinerate vanitas

    O the flow of credulity gushing from public artifice!

The first days took my breath away my golden hair (not yet dolled up with gold dust) my princely chest and the athletic rest of me—a delight for the girls and boys   Clarions carve the air into silver trellises as I drive by glimpsed in my plumed helmet faster and faster to tell everybody here I am beyond the limits with my secret of horse power

I remember the long journey to Rome and the drama of it People waving   Me glorious   My prick stiffened in the surge of their happiness   Little old bowlegged men doffed straw hats and wept   Donkeys brayed urinating on the cobbles of Aquileia   Mountains streamed with milk   Mother!

What was it—the first sight? I had fallen asleep bumping over the big stones   A headache blinded me And then the misty city

    The smells   Vision of my visceral futures: Rome godforsaken heirloom   My inherited economic shit! And sunlit so as to seem imperishable

Fourteen I had been when I saw the ear of wheat being brandished in bony fingers at the end of the dark tunnel Cleverly later I put my lips to the source to chew and snuffle Egypt   I made fashionable the Serapian Mysteries   Not a bad thing to know what figures the gods have cut in imagination if you propose to simulate being the only one of them who frightens the shit out of ostriches

My distended groin? Galenian prigs put serious faces on: a hernia

    I tell you now it was a pretend prick made of pigskin a permanent hard on

Unco trahatur   Let him be dragged by the hook Fancy this: able only to put one face on at a time My mother she had a dream

Gladiators—I was left-handed and my blade was the sharp one although my tongue was barbarian (Viennese with a glint of Serbian)—My gladiatorial displays I staged first for the feast of the Hidden God but that godless plebs   Sweat and uniforms— Everybody too far gone to notice   Saturn: Shit on you

Three hundred concubines and three hundred florescent boys— ghosts of Nero and under his coffered banquet ceilings a great golden belly buried beneath a mass of roses stuffed through square cofferings by the fingers of slaves   —   down among the silver salt shakers   —   Nobody noticed

Universe of power regulated by desire and ancestors: that should have been the balance bestowed by the boys and concubines
Wrong: I turned the whole caboodle into toys   I mistook the beauty of power for the real thing and even dressed as a woman to turn it (turn what?) inside out and upside down   Herculean me Me proprietor of several hundredweights of terrified absorbent flesh   My transcendental eiderdown of sucking mouths and mysterious hairless gums   Wrong: I wanted to see what was buried alive in every hapless shred of flesh

There were lagoons there were snow peaks northward my frontier father I was born to be seventeenth emperor but the first ever to be born porphyrogenitus they reminded me as the iron shod wheels crushed lizards on the big stones

The Pannonians   Combat! Thwong of arrows hitting I loved
deeply most but never the after-prattle of polite meditations

    Dear papa you were talking only to yourself and have I let
you down?   Or did I do what you neglected to do with your
prohibitive purple brains godalmightying a hidden sin?

Probably I perished in a recreation room I spewed the poison all
over the fingers of Narcissus   Narcissus! he could hardly get a
grip on my windpipe

Poor twin my brother what fun you missed

Poor twin you went down into the depths never to see the world
as absolute abominable surface

I took the surface and shook it like a sheet of sea to gather in my
arms the monsters and wrecks as they tumbled out of it

You did not take away my toys

I turned the world we never shared into my toy but totally

Look now I captured footless men and had them wrapped in ban-
dages so like snakes they squirmed across the red tesselated floor
while I shot at them sliteyed   with   arrows   Me

    Another coward wrapped in bedclothes

It was the speed I wanted   In the footless scripts of slaughtered
philosophers measure exists very slightly

Slowness—imbeciles drag their feet to rostrums across the senate
floor   Marble slabs have been discoloured by centuries of spit

The red serpent moves not so but fast

Into my hair I sprinkled scales of the golden slow serpent to see what might conceivably happen   As usual I was gambling

Nothing happened   My brother how could you have dared to be mortal?

My mother before you died I heard you say there was this dream you were raising your arms you whispered

Before you were born I dreamed I gave birth to snakes

Fruit Bringers

The bringers of fruit have in truth no easy time of it

Their bringing of fruit hinges on their luck or judgement regarding the moment

Two moments past the one regarded and it is too late for the fruit they bring contrariwise they must know of the nights through which the fruit grows and if the fruit can endure one more night before being picked they have to let it go through that night

In heavy troughs they bring the fruit and must again take regard that it is not even slightly bruised

These troughs are soaked in the exudations of ancient fruits their walls are notched and inside or out they have a luminous worn look that comes from their being piled one on top of the other like far mountains when empty in the fruitless time or the walls have been dented simply by pressures when fruits fill the troughs to the brim

Sometimes over the troughs full of fruit Serpolnica hovers with a spectre of her victim in whose mouth her beak is fixed and pecking she drinks his blood

Serpolnica touches with her wings the blue or orange fruits that brim to the edges of the troughs

As long as she flaps and sucks her victim becomes shallow being emptied of blood but filled with hubris

One way or another he turns against himself in prejudice and righteousness and upon himself directly or vicariously he aggresses in a manner not conspicuously monstrous

There is not one fruit brought by the fruit bringers that can mitigate the horror of that destruction or avert the necessity of it

If the victim of Serpolnica should take one fruit from the trough she will force it down his throat and suppressively he chokes on it

His golden breath serpent curls up and his pride swells crimson

Stained crimson now his cosmos a culture flowers rooted in his willing not to raise into his thought a radical guilt scripted into him by the splinters and drummed into him by the dyadic throb of his cracked universe

The fruits are one and many but the victim is torn and mangled with tumultuous varieties and severed amid times whose order he knows not

The fingers of the fruit bringers are scarred and freshly nipped by the shears they must use to separate the fruits from the branches rescuing them from the purlieu of the putrid nest in which hideous hybrid Serpolnica crouches in wait and idleness

The victim's fingers are not scarred or nipped he struts about in his cap and uniform and writes death lists in any time he can spare with fingers that are softly domed dreading to touch the fruit or the troughs they are the fingers of an avarice bent on shiftily deviated self-destruction

The victim's feet are swollen from his strutting in the boots that are built to crush the fruits they stamp on

But creation is a making and in this making only began a breaking and a mixing for the first troughs were smashed as the first fruits were showered sidereally into them and in the smashed troughs the serpent breath struggled not to be extinguished in the juice that oozed

There is evil still to be met not a separate substance but a mixture of placid pride and violent aggression in the new trough of the victim's will-to-self and that mixture engages with a malevolence an objective malevolence reddening somehow and wrong in every perfect order of things

At sunrise the fruit bringers feel on their flesh how tender is the breath which models it

For a moment they stop on their way to the fruits and enjoy the air they breathe

Cherry and pear and grape and apple receive their substance from the air and give it back in glowing rounds and ovals eventually on tables between faces

On a flat mountain top there is one table across which an animal is laid for the glory of everlasting germination a table carved from the rock of the mountain

Down the slopes of the mountain are to be seen pathways coiling around caves out of whose most hidden hollows great bears have wandered to make room for torchlit images

Auroch bison and soon horse we shall draw up from the hollows on sensitive coppery fingertips guided by rifts and folds in the rock

Further down the slopes on every side there will be temples and towns Greek or Tibetan huts and terraces and sometimes a quincunx of Persian fruit trees and a tower on a toft until the distance plunging forward flourishes banks foundries and mills military barracks and county court houses coastal or inland smoke infested teeming cities obviously where the poor would perish vulnerable and like children were they not programmed to entertain spectres of prosperity which spin their beliefs on occasion to loosen the hobbles of their suffering

And on the killing table the animal's throat stretched between knife and bowl is a tunnel or it is a bridge between us and what we most fear

We dream that the recipient of our fear wishes no harm being weightless and indeed imponderable whereas we know that like the walls of troughs we are made to carry substance and stain

When the carcass of the animal is tossed into the trough that stands always ready though hidden under the serpentine folds of the killing table we can breathe again

Now heaped in the trough are fruits that can be brought in and the fruits will brighten the home

On their way through twilight the fruit bringers stop for a moment

Singly they stand on their twilit mountain pathway feeling on their flesh how tender is the breath which models it

["Fruit Bringers" concludes the extracts from *Serpentine*]

Bivouac

Among the Polish Chassidim, perhaps among the Chassidim generally in Eastern Europe, it was prohibited to leave a book open in the village reading room. A sacred book, that is. Interfering forces might invade it, or escape from it.

A shadow might, otherwise, cross the open pages. The shadow might distort the features of a divinity which inhabited the pages, at once hidden and open. Or an expression on those features might run wild in the world, unmediated by any mind, the reader's, who sat there in his cloak being bothered by his fleas.

The word desired to be dulled. If not by the mind of this or that reader, with or without fleas, then by the clapping shut of the book. Otherwise the pneuma might break out and be at large, tigerishly among the furrowed desks, or hopping mad in the muddy or sunbaked little village streets.

The book had covers to shield its pages from mud or sunlight. Not even fingers had any title to cross the track of the word. The covers also existed to contain the scorching majesty of the word. At least, a risk was set aside. Who knows, the majesty might otherwise choose to spill out as idiocy and make havoc, or too much heaven, among the huts.

It was also an offence to place one open book on top of another open book. The charms of the pneuma were inviolable, transcendental.

The light shoots shadows into this room, across the pages of books and a few squares of Philippino reed carpet. Somehow I love it so. Outside, the trunk of an elm spells out a green shadow across blades of grass, the quiverings of which can only be detected if you take the time to watch, if you truly care, if you quiver a bit yourself. The grass blades tilt at an inexplicable mass of angles. Their tips ought to be points, but actually are bitten off, because every so often I try to mow the shadows down and the mower's cruciform blade rips across them. Underneath the mower's metal casing the momentarily unseen, as grass, suffers this.

No matter. A sheet of paper on the desk surface carries the print of the insect screen, a tight cross-hatching. This keeps the little winged demons out and holds a whiteness in. Nothing written contradicts the self-sufficiency of the word; its complex force, noted only in various proximate oscillations, disdained by the flea, unapparent in action, otherwise in hope, is a fiction so threatening that we devise our most dazzling footwork to pull a little fruit out of the teeth of disaster.

Here, too, on this bitter grass near dusk I saw the cicada come into being. First it had made its long journey up a perpendicular tunnel to the earth's surface; the cicada itself had lubricated the tunnel with a juice it exuded through its protective pupa. Now, inside the bronze pupa, which was crisping, a general shiver began to happen. An infinitesimal foot prodded a hole in the pupa, then another foot. Gradually the head was coming out, then the body, forwards, but for twenty minutes it made a lunge, rested, lunged again. Its moment of emergence was so prolonged that it could hardly be seen emerging. The motive and the power behind this effort—barely imaginable—I felt them in my groin as a sensation between craving and fright, then in my throat as a taste, brandy and pepper.

Finally, mute and dull, an oval pellet had shrugged the pupa off. The pellet put a leg out, soon another leg. Its back was turning emerald, then golden emerald, with wings that lay flush with the pellet, exceedingly frail, then larger, unfurling into twin networks of golden emerald filigree tracery. And the head, with eyes, had woken up, was turning this way and that way; now the wings could move and lift. The cicada glowed as if dusted with a pollen out of which, for the sake of argument, the breath of a beyond conjectured the world's first agile anatomies. Pristine forest contracted to the volume of a singing bird's egg. A fiery drop of universe at the other end of a tunnel through time.

So I lay down on the grass and put an ear to it. I was expecting the wings to rustle and give off a melodious twang, faint as the last echo of a Jew's harp in an Egyptian burial chamber.

Then it simply wasn't there. From high up in an elm its first ancient cackle fizzed into the onset of dark.

The Image

When they finally got around to where they had begun, it wasn't there any more. This was because they'd strung it out behind them. What had been a chariot of fire had become a rickety old wooden wagon. Losing its parts as it bumped along, wheels breaking, then dropping off, the rest of it a carcass of broken axles, bleached boards, rusted prongs and rotted leather cinches, it had eventually, without anyone noticing when it happened, disconnected itself, then vanished into thin air. It would have made not a scrap of difference if someone had been delegated to keep an eye on it, down the years. They never should have hitched it up, to be hauled behind them, in the first place. So now they looked around, checking the latitude. Forgetfully they wondered where it might have gone. Might they have miscalculated their position? Had they drifted or been driven off course? There had been hazards, they could have been driven off course; they could have drifted, there had been spates of negligence. But no, they had arrived at the exact same spot, this was where they'd begun. There were no signs of the four rivers, no views of the mountain. As for the temperate climate some of the old hands had spoken of, now there came over them a blizzard, biting cold, now the withering oven heat of the desert.

3

From Earth Myriad Robed

1

Why do I hide from this? I see two sides of what I hide from. On one side a sheet of flame. On the other side a violet horn or the horn of a violet (sharper ears might figure which) would have to envelop no secret oil, no quintessence, but a leg of lamb. Then the obstacle flies apart. Out of this horn a pit is made, and the pit exhales a sizzle and three puffs of smoke. But in Madrid a great lady sits, back straight, on her terracotta throne, and she is on both sides. From her, too, I have been hidden. I was hidden from her slow phantom pace through her costumes in history, from the shock of her arrival—from the contraction of her excavated splendour into the clay, this instant. What hid will not be me if only I can touch, without breaking it, a single contour of the uncontainable.

2

Most probably the cook built it with forethought. The scheme haunting his mind might have been Praxitelean, but he fattened that scheme with fierce Turkish caprice. The skeleton sparkled in the depths of his daydreams and a two-pronged plot, just as probably, rose to the forefront of the cook's mind when he balanced his resources against the fortune he might pocket, once his caprice could be made flesh, fully apparent.

The indoor aspect of his restaurant bore on its lintel an inscription in bold Latin capitals: TURKISH KITCHEN DELICATES FIŞIS AND KEBAP. Outside there was dusty space enough for a flock of goats. Here he shook sackfuls of cement into a revolving iron egg. Here he hosed water into the egg for to make a heavy cement paste. With a shovel he turned the cement until it was hardening. Then did he create with it a circular pond to contain water deep enough for fişis therein to outlive the blaze of day. Therefore into the centre of the pond he plunged a pump to circulate the water and to cool it as it flowed. Now he constructed a raised channel with more cement. In the form of a square he constructed it, to frame the dusty space, his kitchen, water chuckling as it flowed anticlockwise along the channel contained by the low walls he clapped into shape with a board. Not otherwise had aforetimes lavish Aegean air circled columns in the peristyle of a temple, to cool the violet interior, where dwelled, ever fresh, in his happiness, at his repose, the god.

Then came the long branches of eucalyptus trees, for the cook did send forth a throng of boys to gather branches from the shore, weathered branches, none thicker than a boy's wrist. And they did gather many; that throng of boys barefoot gathered many and laid them for him in the dust. Now did he trim the branches and he did prop them one against another and he did fix the uppermost twigs and lock them together like the antlers of Hittite stags, and he spaliered the branches on a tilt to support, across a sloped continuous ridge, two long strips of plastic guttering, one above the other, the lower strip concave, the upper strip flat, as a shelf for flasks of orange and lemon juice. Between these gutterings, just above a man's height, he lodged eight empty plastic bottles on their sides, not all of one same capacity, no, but none less than a gallon bottle. He did then perforate each bottle, top and base, so that, once he had coupled the bottles, water soon would flow from one into the next, the first or eighth being the largest and blue, the others being without colour save for their red screw tops. Experimentally then did he let water into the blue bottle and it flowed, through the other seven, at various velocities, none too fast, finally to gush from a spout, made of a shining shoe horn, back into the circular fishpond. Now did he verily set the pump to work and with a great splutter the circuit sprang to life. Water pumped from the pond flowed along the framing channel of low walls and rose by its own motion and pressure into the blue bottle, chugged through the other seven bottles, and dropped back down the shining shoe horn spout into the pond again.

There was also a shade tree set not far back from the blue bottle. To the stout trunk of this tree he did now fasten with clamps of lustrous tin a vertical neon tube, for the shedding of light upon the scene, when twilight should have descended. And he tucked an insulated flex, black and thick, between the tree trunk and the neon tube; all the way back to the roof of the restaurant he then did run the flex in a loop. Out of the flex he teased the wires of fine copper and from these he did hang half a dozen fairy lights, red, yellow, and blue, for now too the electricity could flow, not, he hoped, intermittently, as is its habit thereabouts, but steadily, so that with a certain aurora the fairy lights would sponge the smoke and dust of his arena.

Hard by his cooking pit in the dust he did hang a bell from a spike, and to this bell he tied a cord, the other end of which he fastened somewhere else, so that from almost anywhere in his arena he could pluck the cord and ring the bell. Across the dust, his centre of command, next he did trundle a big tin box with a turning spit in it, and afterward he set beside it with a loud clink, like that of an armoured man bounding into the saddle, an icebox containing a squadron of tincapped beverage bottles. Swigging vigorously from one of these he swung his arms, lifted and stamped his feet, thus and thus; so did he school his waiters not to trip but to skip or pirouette across the walled water channel at his bell's behest. As in a bastion there he now stood, plucking on his cord. Like acrobats the waiters bore aloft to his guests their flashing trays of food and drink, and his guests were ravished to be served nocturnally by such nimble acrobats.

Then did he put on his hat, not stiff and tall like the hat of a hotel cook, but flat and floppy, almost like the hat of a sailor. He took in one hand his long knife and with one stroke severed clean in half a lamb's backside; and anon with his long fierce fork he pronged into my mouth a lamb's testicle, hot from his grill, a gift. He waved his net into the fishpond and pulled a fat fish out, the length of a cubit, a sea trout, and the fish writhed in the net. Its glittering flesh was firm and cold to my touch, and all the while woodsmoke poured from his pit into my nostrils I could taste times out of mind; I saw a web of wrinkles run across the gong-smooth face of a nomad girl and turning into a tiny globe the solo hoot of an Andalusian owl; in a bellshaped, windshook, goatskin tent I lay and heard breath quicken, faster and faster the thump of coupling.

In the second or seventh plastic bottle the cook had housed a young turtle. Gazing far into the night, measuring his mighty words, he did prophesy that when the turtle was grown so big, so big, then would it burst its bottle, then would come the moment, the countertrigonometrical moment, at which every particle he had raised into manifestation would in a flash attain perfection and so melt away, retrieved by the infinite. For then, too, the insulation of the fairy light flex, burned through by the neon's gentle heat, would perish, the shade tree would explode in a sheet of flame and everybody would be electrocuted. Yet for that moment the blaze would everywhere transfigure the night, even far out at sea, so nobody would mind: the glory of the world when it ended would have no end, and if people grieved at all, they would grieve only during that one moment, haply on account of the turtle being boiled to a turn with nobody there to eat it.

3

Rope sole of a razouteur. Dust beaten out of it. A puff of dust beaten out of a rope sole in a small French hotel, old oak beams overhead. In the puff of dust, vestiges of a village dancing floor. A dancing floor in the dust in a land soaked in blood. The features of Elif: mop of tight black curls, dolphin eyebrows, immense dark eyes, small straight nose, her breath from lips parting. Elif in her satin dress, pale golden satin with a blue sash. And the pounding of the music, in the village dust, the puff of dust gone, Elif gone, into the smoke.

The moment of the pigeon when it hovers in the white zenith of a fountain, splashed, uncontainable, the moment of the pigeon. The moment of the wave when it crests. The moment when the wave peaks, mountainous, and orchestrates its prisms to catch the flying light.

The straight back of Elif dancing, all ten years of her, the milling motion of her hands, prints of her bare feet in the dust. A full moon had risen, its globe slowly flew over the distant headland. Smoke from the fire, woodsmoke. The moment of the fat when it spills into embers and the smoke went up, a white flock of smoke, when the smoke is wool, when the owl hoots, when Elif is a lamb, when she mills her hands, as if winding wool with fingers of spindle, wrists arched like ibis beaks.

The throne she sat in was of wood and canvas. She sat in it on the far side of the fire, chin in hand. At a sign she flew across dust between the young men dancing and back again holding in each hand an empty beer bottle. Prints of her bare feet in the dust, erased by the stamping of feet in razouteurs. The throne she sat in was terracotta or maybe stone. She sat with her back straight, wearing a pale gold satin dress, for tonight, the moment when it was tonight, she had not remembered to wear her Ishtar headscarf. And as she flew again across the dust of the dancing floor, she held in each hand a foaming beer bottle.

I had not made any sign to her, but now she stood near. She spoke, at first with a little smile, in surges, at times in leafy whispers, now and then with cries, low but sharp, apparently in a gibberish she was inventing, but always as if it was a great adventure to speak. Some phrases I heard as Greek, others as Turkish. Several sounds I must have misheard, glossing them as English, but her voice drew them up, I thought, while she sang them out, from an origin as indistinct as Hurrian. As she spoke she pointed a finger, this way and that.

-Tais da efendim (so she said, standing near)
bu ghejeh
ti theleis ti theleis efendim
surieyebilir musunuz yakoondala

-oosa ana tanta asnula kyriye
ishmek ishki inghiliz tek ort poro
tek ort poro yabanchuh . . . ti theleis?

-aire kai philia
aire kai kypris
kuruk chok su
kuruk adam efendim

-Poompanul
poompan simi not

-him father fall down rock
sky him all hurt
nunca nunca

-ek te homileo
ek te midolor homileo
lütfen bu yazar
midolor yazar midolor insan dolor

-nehden nehden selene
io nata ikon elithosiniu
sema athanato sema polychrono
io nata io nata chabuk oosa
ana kai roon . . . ula roon . . . kai karanlik
yok palas . . . tek lokanta poro

Here she ran off across a corner of the dancing floor, vanished into an invisible room behind the canvas throne, and soon she was coming back through the smoke with a bowl of ice and another bottle of raki. She set them silently on the table and for moments she stood and looked, tilting her head, and did not speak, did not move. Then with three fingers forming a little trefoil-like triangle, once and lightly she struck the silver Berber talisman on my chest, and she was whispering again:

–baba
baba ti linos mi linos . . . halk müzik
tok asnula singtok
singit rhythmon dalul danstokala
tok thether baba . . . ti linos . . . benim müziyim
thayat awa biles singis binot killet
binot killet . . .
ne akshamleyin ne de sabahleyin

And then her lips closed and she was gazing at the sky. Her throat moved as if she were swallowing, and when she looked at me again she was saying

–dans kuklon
kuklon dans

–lütfen bu yaz . . . bu yaz

–sikilos efter poh . . . seeyin
ahas longas yulif . . . shine

–shimdi gitmem lazum

And she did have to go, her father called to her; huge faces lit by candle flames change their shapes, people feasting sit at long tables in a semicircle, and she is running among them, carrying plates of lamb and fish and cabrito, keeping the glasses full.

Stamping of the feet and stretching the arms out, hand on a hip and hand in the air, the click of the fingers has to perpetuate something, a form, a throb from the footsoles touching the dust and rushing a wave up through the midriff into the shoulders, darkening the blood contained by the domes of the fingertips clicking brushed by the ball of the thumb where from the centre printed in skin tissue the spiral branches out, flesh to its limit carries the pulse and the dance measure remembers a labyrinth, even though we dance rough, whooping and hooting, the land is soaked in blood, the circle is broken and we stumble only fractions of it . . . So that was why these peoples dance in a circle, even two by two inviting memory of a circle—otherwise they might totter singly away, stringing out, lost forever in the distances of Asia, as others are lost in individuality. And there was a tomb far off, brooding vacantly; more near, undiscovered, a seashell had evolved from its node. A bud of rose, a tomb's peaked lid, I remember these, for now the moment of the pigeon makes the twin peaks of Elif's upper lip more than those alone. More now than purely thoughtful she came back, just once, she came back and chose to give me her hands. I would have heaped them with apples, but none grow there. I would have given her a flock of silky black tinkling goats, a box of stories and sketchbooks and pencils, rolls of embroidery, bushels of wheat, her school fees, an orchard I would have given her, a family of ponies in it, but, as it is, I take her suffering with me, and stupidly I tell her "Ya no hay remedio," for a wind in reverse, enormous cyclone, pulls her backwards into the future, pretty soon its teeth will have torn her wings off. Hearing behind her the howl of that wind, Elif has become an outline against a rose trellis, a figure unwinking, mantled, enthroned, in a faraway tomb frieze, and now I'm gone, the dust is nowhere, Elif nowhere, stretching her arms out. The dust, with her long gaze she has fathomed it.

4

The shadow of abstraction lifts from the writing. It is joined soon by the shadow of emotion. The shadows mix, penetrate one another, and obliterate everything, everything except the sound of writing. This is not the clatter of keys, not the yawns of the mouth mouthing words that call to be written. She had told me, Elif had told me, *bu yaz*, write this down. You don't yawn in the face of an Elif; she had said her sorrow is the people's sorrow, *insan dolor*.

As the shadows lift and mix, another phrase is obliterated: *tek ort poro*. I hear it again and am being told—This place is a limit, a threshold. To the sound of writing I must reduce that limit. The sound is not the scratching of a head, not the creak of a chair, not knees cracking. A dust devil spins over an oblong of flowers which wait to be named. Never heard a dust devil sound like that before. A dust devil spinning over bushy oblongs of flowers waiting to be named.

So the male imagines that he constructs, but finally a negative will, till then secret, pops out. Protective the female stands in the circle of dust, juggling oranges; she cups a hand and fields with it the fierce male shots, to add one orange after another to her circus of oranges. Has Ahab heard the scream of Queequeg dying? Ahab has heard the scream and peglegs below deck to discover, tattooed over Queequeg's body, the map of a whole tribal universe. Suddenly Ahab has discovered this universe in the scream too. He brandishes his whalebone cane, shakes his repaired leg, orders his ship about, the China Seas are soon behind, the distances disappear, and instead of a whale it is oranges for Ahab. He has arrived in Valencia, he will spend the September of his life juggling oranges, more and more of them, standing in a dusty square. While Queequeg, recovered, tosses oranges to Ahab, Ahab juggles them, to re-enact for pleasure the whole tattoo inscribed in Queequeg's skin. It is the sound of writing. The sound of writing is the whizz of the oranges, the swish of flails beating flax, it is the thud of feet which dance for the life of Linos, so she said, so Elif said, on the threshold, and for the bondage of Linos to death, of which she said nothing. So we speak of linen and bond. So we do scratch the air until, out of it, come the shouts of the Great Shining Cook of Dalyan, in response, giving no mercy, to the whisper of a spirit in Patara.

The Turkish Rooftops

Turkish country people like to sleep on rooftops. In bowers made of dry leaves or in nests of reed they can be found sleeping in the night or during the day. Village houses have one ground floor where in rooms framed by divans families gather, having first taken off their shoes, on or around rugs of many colours, as close as possible to their earth. On the flat rooftops they sleep as close as possible to their sky. Inside the house, they take shelter. But their resourcefulness, generally, is epitomized in the way they ply, without fuss, between the interior and the exposed aspects of the house. Upon the Euclidean geometry of the house—a cellular cube with a flat lid—is mounted another, unstable geometry in which volumes of whatever description fold like breaths alternately in and out. For all the clutter to be found on it, the rooftop signifies The Uncontainable—to Ἀχωρήτον—as if the purpose of bodies might be to pick away the contradiction, opaque or luminous, of their skin, thus to be unhoused.

Or is it the purpose of bodies to lean so far out that they can read what is inscribed upon their skin? For on almost any country rooftop the bower is ringed, the surface checkered, by variously significant utensils. Turkish country people like to have their tools and the products of their labour arrayed around them, even in sleep. Also laundry hangs there, drying. In pots of earthenware or tin there will be flowers growing: on trumpet vines flowers of startling blue open at first light, close again in the baking heat of noon, open again if ever the onset of night cools the air. The flowers are sprinkled early and later with water from hosepipes that Turkish people flourish at all hours to settle the dust. On the rooftops, too, there is dust. It has to be hosed away, every so often. Every so often, no less, a cat has to be frightened away, with a shout and a stamping foot. Not so the singular immobile objects. What is this assemblage of zinc barrels, two or three, supported by a metal frame? What is this tangle of rods? On a neighbouring rooftop, across the dusty potholed street, can that actually be the driver's cabin of a delivery truck? That curly object on yet another roof is definitely a tuba, for many years unburnished, left behind by a passing army. And even further off, between this rooftop and the distant temple, you can identify the fresher ruins of a sewing machine.

History has swept across the Turkish rooftops all too often. Utensils live their life still uncongealed; certain other objects, not yet dust, are not really débris but relics, relics jettisoned by hordes on horseback, Macedonian footsloggers, Hittite infantry, and a dull glow still envelops them, forgotten though their origin and use may now be. Soon it may even be forgotten that this miniature Byzantine cathedral, with its towers and cupolas, was borne from street to street on the back of a man who for a coin or two dispensed cups of water from it.

A staircase ascends to the rooftop. It is attached to an outside wall. The stairs are of brick, whitewashed, not very wide, often in fact quite narrow, so that if two people were to meet near the top, one going up and the other down, one of those two people would have to flatten himself against the wall and take a deep breath, or the other might topple off the outer edge and crash through the vine trellis that overshadows a small patio below. (Overshadows, but there is more to it: as summer advances, the grapes fatten in their clusters, innumerable silhouettes of leaf, grape, bird or branch of lemon tree engulf the patio and disperse intricate mobile designs across its floor.) In any event, there is no handrail on the outside edge of the staircase. Seldom will you find two Turkish people, either, flattening themselves against the wall or plunging side by side through the trellis. There is a code and the code is observed. Ascent or descent is accomplished without hurry by one Turkish person at a time.

Buckets, parts of cooking stoves, donkey saddles, lengths of rope, piping, sinks, scythes—if you were to survey, on foot or with a telescope, the rooftops of an entire village, you would find a certain constant mass of more or less identical objects, but also a fringe of original and unique objects. The presence of the latter must signify, surely, this or that degree of variance from the norm to which this or that rooftop denizen has risen by dint of enterprise. Not every rooftop has in its repertory of objects a tangle of rods, a paraffin lamp, or a potted oleander. But in very hot villages the bower is a constant. It will be so situated that the least breeze makes the leaves rustle or reeds whisper. Every bower will rustle in the least breeze, so keen is the bower constructor's perception of the sky, so precise the attunement of his imagination to the sky's whims.

The assemblage of barrels mounted on one another in their frame is a water supply. Heated by the sun, the water gushes down (either on the roof or after passing through a pipe into the interior of the house) for a body to be washed; usually the intimacy of the interior is preferred, except by the rudest of travellers who have been welcomed, guests on the rooftop. Nobody can remember what the tangle of rods is, but still it has its place up here, perhaps merely as a ghostly presence to be stepped around. Or else it is a sky trap. When you wake up among the trumpet vines you might find a piece of the sky, nocturnal animal, snared in it, still groaning, shuddering a bit. Perhaps that is what my grandfather found. Why else would he have refused one day to strap his Byzantine water cathedral to his back and the next gone off to Izmir in search of a ship?

Remember how, in Cézanne's paintings of Mont-Sainte-Victoire, the mountain changes its clothes, sky its diagonals that shine or rain down upon the roof of the mountain. Dense oil or transparent watercolour, the picture itself is this threshold of contact between orders of objects, present as rock, represented in the picturing act as liquid, remember. Well, every bower envelops a low platform made of wood.

A thin mattress is laid over the wood. Over the mattress is laid a woven rug, and cushions are placed for the sleeper's head to rest on; perhaps a thin, if not threadbare, blanket will also be there. A thin blanket, brown or grey. A threadbare blanket. Dust billows out when you shake it. A blanket.

Optimally there will be a mosquito net. A delicate white cocoon, folded back by day its flaps are released at night and secured by strings. Probably many Turkish babies have been conceived on rooftops; tired women refresh themselves in these bowers; in their nests old men look up at the moon and recover hope.

On some Turkish rooftops you will see oblongs of concrete from which steel rods stick out, some askew, some perpendicular. The oblongs are positioned symmetrically, but the rods go every which way, and some do say they are an eyesore. Why are they there? Is it to anchor a new storey eventually to be built over the rooftop, so that the enclosure of any one present rooftop will lead to the unfolding of another, higher up, even closer to the sky, even cooler than the one the new storey will have enclosed, and so up and up, like a squared ziggurat? Some say the new storey will never be written, I mean built, but that Turkish people cling so fondly to their idea that nothing can ever be finished, nothing achieved, that they leave the oblongs there, with rods sticking out, to remind them always that life is impermanent, it is improvised, therefore they imagine rather than complete the upward extension, so the oblongs of concrete are ritual supports, not for new rooms but for ancient and compulsive imaginings, the forgotten past has its ruses, mischief in the air, now where was I? Others again say that if an addition is evidently projected but not yet finished you avoid paying tax. Even the last explanation admits a principle. It is a principle pervading many features of life on Turkish rooftops: let every matter lie open, the boiling stuff of existence stays greener if no lid is put on it, earth calls to its lover the sky, sky calls back to earth, the transparency of a few dashes of intense blue or peach in a water-colour mountain may tomorrow condense into an oil colour so richly glowing that the mountain, tutored by the painter, in whose visions at first light, torrential but caught behind closed eyelids and configuring of their own accord, rock was turned into air, is shipped on its way apparently to Mohammad.

From such a rooftop you hear many voices. Night or day, human voices, animal voices. A rooster is crowing. Chickens thoughtfully cluck. A donkey brays. The little owl chants its one and only note, sometimes trilling it. Frogs instruct the stars to relax, relax. Out of nowhere a momentary song has floated into and out of the mouth of a girl in the street below. Or the timber trucks thunder by, the minaret emits a gravelly voice, that of an illtempered old man, Allah Allah, enraged to have been woken up, he is reaching for his sword, Akbar.

Toward nightfall, listen for the drum. An old drum is being thumped among the huts, under the eucalyptus trees, a clarinet has joined it, playing a wiry tune, spiral, to the monotonous beat of the drum it adds a melody, a catch.

Somewhere down there, people are streaming toward the huts, in serious clothes, wizards in peaked caps, young men with fresh haircuts. Always the drumbeat, still the clarinet's catch. With or without your telescope—if with it, then be sure to wipe the oil or watercolour off its lens—you see the drummer, a brown old village man, made of olive wood, and the stick in his fingers never misses a single beat of the three it is capable of. The clarinet player is young, his lungs sepia with nicotine, but he is blowing without let-up, the catch is attractive. Duly the crowd is ushered through a gap in the fence just before the Pepsi sign. People push through, the drummer will drum for them, the clarinetist blow for them long after all have settled in their ring around the dance floot. There, another music, more densely enormous, has now begun, and the wedding feast explodes, women dancing first, soon joined by uncles and fathers, finally by capering young men with arms outspread.

By this time you are with them, but as you spread your own arms look back to your rooftop. Hearing in contradiction the two musics, one dense, one transparent, you now conceive of the rooftop not as their analogue but as yet another threshold, altogether distinct, at which resemblances vanish, vanishing points of brilliant green and cool rose converge on the breathlike peril of substance, the deep ground of their volatility: a platform shrouded by leaves dried ochre by the air.

The Execution of Maximilian

1890 already, or almost, and not later. This is the room. This is where ... Méry Laurent received Mallarmé and Gervex. This is the room in which they were photographed. (Stooping hooded behind his tripod stands either a hired professional or Dr. Evans, Méry's protector, whose diagonal gaze used to rake the interior of Napoleon III's mouth; or else, having shot a last glance into Napoleon's mouth twenty years ago, near enough, Dr. Evans had already quit the scene.) First it is Méry we see, sitting at her grand piano. Her hair looks blacker, sparser than it should; by all reports it was a glossy torrent, honey-colored. We see Mallarmé, his goatee now whitening below his underlip. Standing behind Méry he lunges at something, an emotion, one arm extended low, as if to evoke the buttock absent from all the bloomers. We see Gervex, who leans forward, arms crossed on the back of his chair, gazing at Méry, a grizzled profile, short legs and bony knees in pinstriped trousers. The two big windows are shut. Because there are roses on the piano, it might be Spring. Do these people, with their aching heads, only feel at home in sealed and riddlesome rooms? Deep pelmets overhang mushy drapes of velvet; or is one small window open, after all, for outside, strangely suspended above and behind the small head Méry tilts, coquettish, in mid-air . . . Mexican riffraff in French uniforms are shooting Maximilian point blank. Maximilian stands between two thieves, who are generals and are also being shot by their riffraff with French rifles and French bullets. Maximilian is wearing, while the bullets riddle his torso, a tall sombrero. That is what seems to be going on, that is where the action is, in the air outside, on this dark artistic evening. Back inside the room, everything is contained, except the perfume. In a glass hutch the bric-à-brac is contained; in a heavy damask cloth the piano; contained in heavy frames the diminutive paintings on the panelled wall, many by Manet. Even the sofa is contained in the skin of a lion, the people in their clothes, the mirror in its ornate gilt; and hung over the mirror, so that she may see her beautiful face, a portrait of Méry slopes, blurred, containing in its invisible back an oblong hardly less negative than the azure zero which still haunts, still excites Mallarmé as he lunges, extending an arm. The oil contained in tall brass lamps is so pure, so still, the wicks it feeds ("humects") do not smoke as the rifles are still doing while Maximilian discovers that the Bank of France has decided to drop him. The tallest picture, at which nobody is looking, can be identified by the lion man. Inhabiting the bottom right-hand corner of the only section visible, he scribbles with a white quill an elegy, perhaps for his skin which contains the sofa. Above the disappearance of Maximilian and his thieving generals in puffs of gunpowder smoke floats, or is hooked, a decomposing bird of paradise. Under so many eyelids, the roses on the piano, fresh, presented with a smile by Mallarmé, pretend to be nobody's sleep. They will be trembling when Méry turns back to the keyboard and concludes the evening with a spirited hat dance.

Balzac's Face

On a small-scale map you could identify it, if its name would only come back, the village where at a certain windless moment each year in late June the face of Balzac appears, clearly marked on the plaster of an isolated broken wall. The village is empty now; hollyhocks, fig trees, bushes of weed flourish up and down its six or seven winding lanes. You can walk there: doors are boarded over, windows shuttered, roofs have caved in, but suddenly they will be there, the features of Balzac. His head, exactly as it was caught by Nadar, if Nadar it was, tilts up, the lock of black hair falls across his forehead, a placid but piratical look, accented by the up-tilt, dominates this creation of leaf shadows. It is Balzac to the life, for the moment relieved of his body, and intrepid. Once there was a manor house, but now there's no money in it; its refectory forms a bridge over the narrow cobbled street. Into stone walls on each side, two respectable vertical conduits were fitted, shallow from erosion now, for channelling manorial excrement into the street. No more, at last, as nature consumes culture, inch by inch, in Balzac's nose the whiff of economic shit; nor will the stories of village people swarm in a grand imagination. If masons could be found, carpenters, plumbers, water-diviners, the little houses, shunned even by strangers on vacation, surely they could be restored, but only by an artfully sustained Balzacian enterprise, their heyday recuperated, why not, along with an equilibrium, never chronicled, which embraced their utensils, goats, abbots, alps, and milkmaids. More sensitively than most, the face of Balzac presides over the stricken scene. Contoured by shadows cast by a tree in the afternoon sunlight, Balzac's eager face looks on, with sweeping moustache, eyes secure in their sockets, while the curves of hirondelles, figures of mice, passions of dragonflies, intrigues of startled bats build up to something in his head of shadows. If the wind blows, then the weeds lean over, a shutter bangs, the face is dispersed. A cricket chirps in a kitchen, an old beam trimmed with a hatchet groans beneath its roof; the face of Balzac waits for the wind to drop and to be seen again.

Cliff's Dwarf

My friend Cliff took to a dwarf in Trebizond. Swaggering out of our hotel we passed behind ranks of men on their knees, at prayer, while all around them traffic whizzed, and then we approached the dwarf. He sprang out of his basket and with his left hand gestured to us to enter his restaurant—a splendid gesture. He also bowed, but only slightly, perforce, him reaching no higher than our stomachs. He was perfectly proportioned, but so small that he lived in a basket, serving only to motion, with his splendid gesture, visitors into the cavern of his restaurant.

My weathered friend did not heed the gesture, but, with an equally good grace, stopped and shook the dwarf's right hand—the entire arm disappeared for an instant inside Cliff's genial palm. "*Hoş bulduk efendim*," he explained, "but we are out for a walk, *geziyoruz*, and perhaps we will gratefully return." The dwarf climbed back into his basket, and we walked on. The next day, the same reciprocal attentions; recognized by the dwarf, Cliff again told him: "*Bügün de biraz geziyoruz*," and back to the basket went his dwarf.

We thought of the dwarf on that second afternoon. Under our sunshade, in one of the tea houses that cover the celebrated square in Trebizond, we exchanged our thoughts. This great forum down to which, through a maze of winding alleys, some very late Byzantine emperors descended from their ramparts, clad in cloth of gold, to review the dazzling Circassian and other maidens; there assembled, all the maidens, especially the Armenian ones, hoped to be chosen as brides, though one alone would be chosen. This celebrated arena: the dragged-out blare of Pontic trumpets, brisk tattoos from kettledrums, the rancid smell of the executioner's moustache as he sucks it, the puff of smoke from the pipe he deposits on the block, the flash of the executioner's sword as he lifts it, the gasp of the throng, the glitter in the eyes of Cliff's dwarf's forefathers. Grinding as it was, that ancient street life, they came to know no other, and flesh for generations absorbed its avalanche of noise so fondly that, far from going deaf to it, or blind to the pulsing hologram of signs it was the skin but not the heart of, desire could finally take no more and had scraped from its echoing barrel's bottom not dregs enough for one last crackling loaf, only enough for a solitary *börek*, frittered, in its basket. O slow decay of the golden haze historians twirling giant locust antennae lacquered over the town! Others, meanwhile, had waited for the barbarians—all the latest books tossed aside, unread; all the puzzles long solved, puzzle contrivers tearing their last few hairs out; what curlings of lips into sneer or pout when noble youths and their nanas, bored with Miss Byzantium ceremonies, cackle anew about fashions the barbarians might bring in, mangling quotations as they poohpooh the pomp of the cavalry, the quibbles of bishops, and stick out their tongues at recently ennobled *nouveax riches* who stand there all agog, there on the great square, while robes rustle in the sea breeze and towers tremble in the noon mirage. Did the barbarians really gnaw the haunches of living oxen for dinner? Did, in their country, chickens run around raw? Did those men wear trousers? Why does the Emperor flit like that through his palace, from window to window, showing the point of his nose now and then, but a nose so accustomed to the smell of blood that it might just as well be the nose of a ghost?

On the third day, Cliff was all set to shake again his dwarf's hand as we passed by, but his dwarf never sprang from his basket. He was not looking at us, and he made no gesture. Cliff's dwarf was miffed.

We paused, but he clove to his basket, and he yawned. That small yawn from Cliff's dwarf dismayed us. Would he leap up, if we passed? With what contortion might he reverse his gesture? Would Cliff's dwarf cuss us out? We knew his voice: it buzzed. Cliff's dwarf's voice was a deep and loud drone, a hornet's voice; or no, none but the concentrated buzz, heard as from some middle heaven, of a thousand years on the street. "*Hoş geldiniz!*" he had droned, "*buyurun. . . .*" and then his splendid gesture. But now, yes, miffed, the dwarf only yawned. As we walked on, he hurtled out of his basket, on his feet in a flash, and we heard him buzz behind us: "Never again will I say *buyurun* to you, nevermore; do you suppose, *messiö*, that times long gone are bigger than me, sweeter than the feasts I bid you to, more important than my yawn? The fire, *messiö*, the sacred fire, you forgot it!" We turned, too late, Cliff's dwarf had hopped back into his basket, not too late to glimpse the grin he tried to exchange with his *patron*, who had bustled out of the cavern into the doorway, hands lifted, shaking his head.

Le Déjeuner

A description of a painting ... has to begin. With an assertion. If, to see this big square painting, you stand on your head—in the Jeu de Paume it used to be permitted—you may see features not otherwise seen. From the top descends a hemisphere of shadow; from the bottom ascends a hemisphere of light. The shadow permeates sparse tree foliage, a French window-door with shutters pinned back to the wall on each side of it, a summer hat apparently hung in a closer tree, a border of geraniums, and a flowering shrub in a footed green box. The light permeates a table, over which a cloth of white linen has been spread, a fruit bowl with a tall stem standing on the table, then a blue coffee cup, it permeates a wine glass, off-centre a silver coffee pot with a looped handle (little echo of the hemisphere, set on a black tray), elsewhere another coffee cup, then a large white rose and a small one on the hither side of the table, at which a trolley stands, a trolley with a basket top, the basket top containing a shallow bowl of fruit, a wine glass, and a brioche from which a slice has been cut.

Shadow dapples the table cloth. The fruit bowl with the tall stem breaks the curve of the table and so is sharply outlined in the middle ground left of centre against the soft orange of the sunlit garden path. Shadow in the upper part of the painting is also lightened toward the right by the white hanging hat and a white exploding rose held against the hat crown by the long black hat ribbon.

The effect of the hemispheres is only marked if you stand on your head. If you do not stand on your head, you will probably see only, or glimpse—boundaries here are so moulded as to suggest, by restraining it, a pressure from the abundance secreted by things, which, if it broke free, would bury everything in a dazzling avalanche of aura—a diagonal from top left to bottom right separating shadowy from sunlit areas, for it passes across the orange path to bury itself in the folds of a white parasol which has been deposited on the seat of a curved and slatted garden bench. A complementary diagonal, and a more quivering one, passes from the bottom left corner, through the tiny easel to which a little squatting boy attends, beneath the table and across a clump of flowers; beyond the flowers it finds two women, between the women a forked green space echoes the dark forked folds of the parasol. This diagonal loses itself in the stomach of the woman robed in yellow, then it reappears, to arrow the short remaining distance up through more foliage and strike the top right corner of the painting.

Happily the crossing diagonals are not so marked as to hint of deletion. Yet there was to have been a lunch and now the brioche is barely nibbled on, there is wine reddening the bottoms of both glasses, the cups are not darkened by coffee. Did the heavy yellow woman interrupt the lunch? Did the slender woman in white, now wearing a formal, turret-shaped and forward-tilting hat, run to meet her and remember while she ran that, Oh, a guest had been invited? Had the slender white woman, now so formal, only minutes ago flung her hat with rapture into the branches—before the heavy visitor rapped twice on an invisible door with an inaudible brass knocker?

There can have been no lunch to speak of, only some commotion.

Suddenly the painter saw the picture, flung his copious linen napkin on the table, shoved his chair back across secret orange gravel he's now standing on, fished his brushes out and began to paint. It was he, too, who disrupted lunch. Now he dissolves into its components the instant of commotion which instigated his insight. He has caught the flying instant as an aura contained in coloured objects, transfixed by two diagonals, and cushioned by two polarizing hemispheres. The picture presents the permanent dance of particles inside the shell of a disruptive incident. No time for lunch.

Two women, two cups, two wine glasses, two roses, a handbag on the bench beneighbours the parasol, the hat ribbon trails two extremities. And the little boy squats on the ground, contentedly alone at his tiny easel; his partner is papa, the painter, a pair of hands at an invisible easel in the most impenetrable fold. The painter, transparent. You see not him but his insight. Sitting or standing, he will have been where you have come to be. A descant.

Another descant: from the depths of a dark Algerian mosque two voices alternating, one broken, old, but gradually swelling, the other, young, streaming from above, Isabelle Eberhardt heard them flash in her as they combined to complete a circuit which discharged in her "almost an ecstasy."

The heavy woman was a disruptor too. The painter deals with her. He paints her as an immobile vast chrysalis of a faintly golden hue. She is no mere marginal part of the web of the picture. The spider painter caught her in his web, his *toile d'araignée*. Also the hat, the incongruous hat hung in the tree, he catches it so deftly that, if you block it out with a hand, the web, for all its shimmering tonal affinities, lacks flourish, has been drained of elasticity.

So the hat was flung up there for joy, not by the lady before the forgone lunch began, not by her, but by the painter, who picked up, from the ground where Delacroix had tossed it, Jacob's hat, picked it up and flung or floated it into the glory of his web, and while sailing upward it was transformed from a well-worn Hebrew shepherd hat, curly-brimmed, heavy with dust and sweat, to become a debonair Val d'Oise summer hat in 1874, from whose crown cascades a wide ribbon, black, but since its ends are fluttering, divided, this black isn't death, it is trousers, with sinuous legs in them, describing the double-step of a dance.

Jacob's angel has been retired—blushing—into the chrysalis with a faintly golden hue.

The story can't be told otherwise than by a seclusion. The disruption of the normal incident, a lunch, can't be accounted for, until in his memory the painter reconstitutes the disruption and imagines, with marks that play across the web from all sensitive angles, seldom in sequence, the impact of an intensity that only came to be lifesize when he saw there was something doubly abundant he'd forgotten.

In the Mirror of the Eighth King

Macbeth sees in the mirror not himself but a succession of kings. Unless memory is playing him false, he sees a future which is not for him.

Startled by this parade of his antipodes, Macbeth, the warlord, a noxious Narcissus, so spellbound by his own image that even when evils he inflicts erratically on the innocent rebound and pierce him, he tweaks them out with his teeth, does not now perceive, in the faraway depth of the mirror being held up to him by the eighth king, the most secret figure.

With wild flowers up to her waist, a child is standing. She looks as if she might at any moment fly up, shimmering, and perch on the ruined tower silhouetted behind her, or on top of the ruined wall, sunlit, to her left, where an ashtree is rustling.

Macbeth is still staring thunderstricken at the mirror, at the figures crowding the surface of it. Double orbs, treble sceptres—among the heirs he will never have there will be emperors, just so long as market forces modernize them.

The child's right hand closes over the head of a wildflower. Her left hand, for a moment the fingers are folded in on her palm. Over her face, half in shadow, plays the ghost of a smile, and a deep, a glowing rose colour saturates her skin.

Egged on by Lady Macbeth, the warlord means to take into his possession all the time to come, make it all in his image, hatched from his will. His person cannot propagate otherwise. He is powerful, but he is sterile. On his sterility, his carcass of a soul, all his power is mounted, thrusting, grunting.

The child wanders around in her Byzantine garden, feeling everything to the quick. She feels how every motion of her small body harbours the morning of the world. She is wearing her aquamarine shirt today; she slipslops along in dangerously pointed black shoes borrowed from her mother.

With a fist the warlord mechanically strikes his brow and he curses the witches who have staged this show of kings. Then he scuttles back to his bunker, where he will rehearse at a keyboard every phrase of his next manipulative oration. It is the one he will deliver tomorrow and tomorrow, while manacled on his knees, before first light on August 19, 1936, after the fusillade, Trecastro now drawing his pistol to give the *coup de grâce*, Lorca shouts in terrified astonishment: "Yo vivo, yo vivo!"

Reaching out on either side, the child has cupped in her fingers the pods of poppies, unless those are thistle heads. But why hold on to anything? It is enough to know by touch what things mean. For the present, you are safe. She stands outlined against the Byzantine wall, rough-hewn masonry, colour of porphyry. Slowly primeval waters moulded all that stone; still awash with them the mirror has not yet cracked under the stone blocks, these wild flowers randomly strike root in it, and the child is busy reinventing the sky, which is here, close. An airstream caught in her aquamarine shirt ruffles them, shirt and mirror; she has danced in a ripple of drapery across the mirror surface, she is mortal. More and more confident her smile tells the world that air can hatch no danger. When she steps out of the mirror into her brief candle time to come, it will flash for her to remember that she flew. Finding no reason to doubt it, she will tell nobody how.

4

Coriolan

Do I have to house myself in this bone? Coming as I do from far away, the bone is too small at first. Too small, but it grows. It grows. Now I have a long domed thighbone and my home is in it. Fingerbone as it might have been, neither headbone nor kneecap, it is a long hollow, snappable as a celery stick, a fish bone, a dead man's bone, of which, having lived around it, or, like a dog, dug it up, you know not where it came from, yet dare not breathe on it.

Inside this bone, there is room. A large room opens in the bone, more room, more. The bone encloses light, yet the light flows through the room. Where from? I have come through a little door and am astonished, as I straighten up, to recognize, all round this oval room of illuminated bone, such windows: are they peep holes? Not even perpendicular frames into which smaller frames of steel snugly fit. Not even the mired glass oblong in the rain-ringed plaster of an attic ceiling, the trap you have to shove aloft with a rusty rod. No: here the windows are perennially open huge flute holes through which winds blow their tunes.

Well, so, seeing such windows, should I have run, shaken by fright, to close them? Instead, I run to look out: and there is the town. Through it a blue-green river flows. I see beside it, far off, an isosceles silhouette. No mistake: a fisherman is standing there. Just then he hooks a shining fish, shining and curly, scaly, striped. He stares up at the window I am standing in. We connect, at an angle, midway along the fishless line between our looks. Then I know I am invited. In his fist, his left fist, he holds an oar, upright; it is not a winnowing fan. An open fire, he hears it crackling beside him, on this shore of the river.

But the room—I had to be in the bone room. What are these coral streaks in the whiteness I am standing on? And these other windows: I float to the next one. Look out—see a country of dense forest, caverns, ravines with familiar tombs carved into towering scarps. Sparkling far off, an ocean. A few white whisks of cloud over there mean that the simoon has come and gone.

So these columns, orange trees in the gardens, walled shadowy lanes, wisps of smoke that rise from holes in tiled roofs, cluster on either side of the river, and the river runs freely to the ocean. Except for the tinkle of goat bells from below, the room is silent, and wait a moment, the splashed coral reminds me of bloods I have seen elsewhere, and then there was no such hush.

Looking out again I hear the single note of a watchman's horn. What pleasure, ah, the pang of it, to smell the animals. Goat and cow, wild pig, the ferret who smells of hay rotting in the sun, the spoiled fruit reek of a puma. I begin to hear voices, now some are murmuring, now some crack into muted sobs, screams without rage, yet the room—open windows, flute breath and all—is far away from all that, and it is clean.

With slow steps, somehow, and between my sharp shoulder blades and beaten down, bent double by sorrow, jaw tightening, lips stretched, neck tendons tight, I cross the floor, drawn to a table. There is a table, made of alabaster, or marble, or crystallized bone.

As I approach it, I see that the table gives off a glow that I have seen before. It is the white cube of rock, veined with red, I saw long ago in an arroyo forking from the north into the Rio Grande, half a day's ride west of Langtry. It is a natural table, on a ledge; back of the ledge, rock shelters, once deep, had been shallowed by time, by weather. This is my table, and it is calling to me. Here, with light falling on the table from the window beyond it, I will be at work, working at what?—and for ever? Off and on—always the view, to spark interest. I tell myself that the fisherman, and there he is again, it is Steve Pollard the mackerel catcher of Cadgwith, will show me, above and below ground, the people in Coriolan, this lost city I despaired ever to find. In the taverns and kitchens, there will be people; secret pastures will open to us when we unlatch gates that are intangible in the depth of time.

I am looking up, the far ravines, the forest, the ocean have not gone away, but all at once I am peering down at the surface of this bone rock table. Here is a golden fish, under a coating that took thousands of years to become hard, yet not opaque. Snail-paced sedimentation on luminous bone; powdered under the pressure of an unknowing that sustains every individual time bubble (each with its own tension, its own air, its own inscrutable vacancy), a substance has been sieved to lacquer the table, to trap the fish. One bright round eye is fastened on me: this fish, clothed in a brocade of curly glittering scales, itching to wiggle, is alive. I am ready, with this knife in my belt, to attack the bone surface, assail the lacquered rock, set the fish free.

Then, in the bone, a script appears, also coated, at first a script written by a child, in separate crude letters, coated as if fluid but crystallizing light had for a long time washed back and forth across it building the layers of rock or of bone, while it constituted impetuously, too, the letters which keep changing, so that the legend changes its code every time you look, the characters themselves changing, now Coptic, now Latin, now Georgian, now Arabic, Armenian, Greek, more and more certain the strokes, less and less decipherable their legend, on account of the mutations. No way, opening eyes or narrowing them, to arrest the flux of the script. Whoever is writing it, the legend, though it is no lengthier than a breath, forbids me to think it a message for me.

What is this? And who is this onlooker who does not know if he is being fooled, thwarted, or waved away?

Surely another glimpse from the other window will break this trance the script has put me in. Pollard is there, he beckons, beckons again urgently, our eyebeams are knit once more, and now he has placed his fish on a grill over his fire. How can he have survived the sixty odd years, the wars, the stupor of our country? From his painted boat, out at sea, feeling the tug, whenever fish lips took his hook, pass from the end of the line into his fingers, he might have caught a thousand shoals of mackerel. Inland now, he won't mind waiting. Didn't they say that waiting is three fourths of a fisherman's occupation?

I cup my hands to my mouth and shout. "Hodié yok!" There is no echo, because there is no sound, and now not the script, which is extinguished, but the scarps are moving with their tombs, moving to encircle the town, or not quite—still there is a gap, to my left, through which daylight has carved a crevasse and I could slip. Can I even find the door and crouch and worm my way through, then run for the crevasse? I know the circle has closed. Even if I could find the little bone door, what's the use? I have lost the knack of effort, am bereft of the vigilance any least effort used to bring. The fury I contained, to keep my eyes open, their motion constant, has left me. The follies, calamities, the partings that broke my sleep, of them no trace by which to measure this drifting off, nothing to hold me through this letting go.

Parthenogenesis in Charcoal

Looking at her he wished that with a look at him she might shorten the smoky distance between the tables.

When she looked, when she turned her head at last and her look met his, he had looked away. An accident? Never mind, he'd known it was too foolish. Do not, he was telling himself, do not obtrude.

Her own concerns were no obstacle; he could feel the weight—and agitation—of scruples multiplying in the impression he had received. Fugitive as it had been, it had made more than a dent; all sorts of shimmerings, inextricably virulent and pure, trickled into it and down, down: the hair she didn't know what to do with, the glint afloat in her eyes, the black locket she wore, the ribbon of horsehair that held it against the skin of her throat, the shape she made out of the arms she had folded, having not much in particular to say, for now, to the fellow facing her at their table.

He looked again; again she looked away, but thought better of it and stole another look, no, she took it, straight on, much as a mustang filly gathers her hoofs and arches, with all grace, over a palisade. He knew then how he might later begin to draw her.

The narrow street, people strolling up and down with their gestures and children. Plaster had fallen off the walls beneath the shutters; unpatched ochre, bare brick. A little tree was lofting its leaves but needed water. And one taller window frame—under it a shelf was secured by bars of iron curled into treble clefs—someone inside must have taken the flower pots in and fastened the shutters. Once they hoisted hay into that room; now, shared by neighbours, a washing line ran confidently across the wall from window to window.

Shadows defining themselves; grafitti scribbled where spaces had been blank; people speaking loud language, then munching on the food they scooped out of dishes; here he was, stuck in the tight stifling uttermost end of the funnel, and gazing back up he could see only straw.

Surely he must by now have a secret feeling for them, insight, not invasive, unless observation had gradually altered sympathy into a certitude, not unwelcome, of his remoteness. You eluded them: how come they still took you unawares? Who but a wizard might tell what muscle tempered their pageantry? And this one: of the right dynasty? If not, or if the legacy had dwindled, that could be rectified; stable dust blown off it, its whispers overheard, straw lifts up an array of golden mobile tubes. Again he set eyes on her.

Not yet two-faced, he supposed, she'll still be wily; through one single feature, if he could isolate it, her complete and distinct system might dance into the open. Zest, this was the motive, so the vague gesture, plied back into each one of them, consolidated afresh as a stark and whirling form, asked not for another life, but to irradiate, to the tips of its wings and talons, this one. O mother, he thought, nymphs, they all start alike and so soon become different. How can It have come to This? Cheekbones, no. Colour, no. The way her fingers stormed through her hair, or, making an oblong fist, brought the crumbs innocuously to her lips.

No. It must be the music coming from inside the tavern. The notes, in twos and threes, mounting, derision in the breath. Only a clarinet. But she had a smile for the sheep, an old sheep which, there and then, bringing confusion, stepped uncertainly across the candle-lit terrace. As it skittered off, she put her hand on the hand of whoever it was, let's not be going just yet? So tilting her head and peering over the interposed shoulder, until she felt herself disappear into his gaze, she could take a long look at him now.

A Polka in the Evening of Time

Henri Toulouse-Lautrec, in a night spot, unflustered, but amused, considering his short legs, his passion for *la ligne*, his being devoured by his perceptions, these people dancing, the turbulence patterning their limbs, the timed closure of the accordion, then the stability of bottles, gaslight shimmering down their necks in which he sees, telescopically, warped by the curves of glass his neighbours' faces, and comparing with those faces his own face, with their torsos his hat—they stamp, I levitate, they slump, I fizz, they're normal, I'm a monster, oh and they have lives before them, mine is a joke—knows that Alexander von Humboldt has explored South America, that Alexander's physique is an instrument fit to contend with the crocodile, the anaconda, rotten food, and fleas.

All the time he is taking notes. What a strapping fellow. Back I go to my butterfly book. Am I Henri? Or Alexander? An absinthe specimen, immense wings, crimped like a woman's at the waist. Notes not pictures infest my book, the pictures illuminate only. I could compose, I could invoke. He took it all down, did Alexander von Humboldt, chewing on his rotten food, his iron beard immersed in mud, howled at by mosquitoes and Amazonians, miscreants all, and swatting a wasp away Henri regrets the loss, in a tributary, of his notes and sketches, of his peace of mind, whose? Who? And whose book?

Ungrumbling Alexander brushes a thousand snags aside. Henri has a cause, too. Henri and Alexander together record a vast, riverine, forested, inhabited province of mother earth, her body firstly, that "mobile perilous thing," upon which they perch, our navigators, riding athwart her stretch marks, their boxed documents swept overboard sign to them: Begin Again. It's life, it's risk, it's it. If Alexander aims to impart original knowledge of it all, all, Henri aims, no less, to fix the singular of sense in which the soul comically throbs. Both love this—and they wonder at the diadem of pearls threaded into the hair of an Empress, dead Faustina, silver in her coin, then a sudden cool ventilating the cabaret, the creak of a cork being slowly twisted up the neck of its bottle, the human eye opening wider in its surprise, the work, huge and hard, of disturbing Necessity, of slipping through Obstacles, on the track of—what?—wingbeats, niceties. For life stops. All its fractions and splendours, they stop. Here we are, the savages. From our tall trees and deep burrows we are watching; we who are not afraid, all the way in, are being watched.

Wahoo, into a hut. Ferapont does not know Henri, Ferapont does not know Alexander. Ferapont is a vigorous old ascetic; his hair is thick, his slippers are dropping to pieces; his coat, long and reddish, is made of coarse convict cloth. He does not speak prose. Ferapont, Henri, Alexander, only one of them speaks prose.

Ferapont speaks riddles. Sees devils. A devil with his tail pinned in the door, over him Ferapont made thrice a sign of the cross. Allegedly the devil died, crushed like a spider, on the spot. Henri Toulouse-Lautrec regretted it: he was wanting, dear mama, to portray for you a devil's tail pinned in a door, but was he then too far away? Said Ferapont, housed in his hut of wood, and curious, as was Alexander, about the birds, "a goldfinch told me a fool would visit me and ask unseemly questions." Ferapont has a back door on which, with spindly fingertips, the Holy Ghost taps, as the beak of a goldfinch might—*nick, nick*. He peers out of his hut. Remote but there, his pulse racing, in the Russian forest atmosphere, the door still creaking on its hinges, he beholds in the winter branches of an elm the crucified Christ.

The Gaze of the Turkish Mona Lisa

I could feel her gaze resting on me, so strangely, lightly, that it would have been inept to return it. She sat diagonally opposite, at a small square table, in this "Iskender Kebap," or Alexander Grill. There she had settled with her sturdy husband and fat (anon hiccuping) son. Close as this family was to me at my identical table, their conversation, scant in any case, was almost inaudible. Me in my buff travelling shirt and white trousers, with my white beard, rather ragged, thinning brown hair, she was taking me in. While she'd been sitting down I had looked at her: a fleshy woman wearing a headscarf that spread across broad shoulders, a nondescript headscarf. Then, in an instant, I had noticed something about her lower lip. As she almost smiled, or pouted, a tiny crease appeared in it, a seamark on a horizon. I remembered the same crease which appeared now and then in Tana Cochran's lower lip, also halfway along the left half of it, whenever she looked rueful but was also taking me in. What sort of a conspiracy might this be?

This Turkish woman's moon face would have looked heavy, too much flesh, if it had not been for her delicate features, the tilted planes of skin which pronounced those features, catching the light as she turned her head. Her eyes were not large, but lazy, inviting intimacy, the skin a rosy brown with a velvet texture, and now a gentle disdain, untainted by any bitterness, haunted her expression.

So she was not altogether submissive, and her face, her barn of a body (on this hot summer evening in an upstairs downscale Iskender Kebap), her body beneath all those swathes of light clothing, stored the woes and waves of a resistance that have for centuries shaped her function in the family—to oblige, but in the worst of times to bite every bullet, to provide at all times from the least resources. I did want to look into her face, wanted to show that I was not indifferent, not an object; but feeling her gaze on me, the stranger—perhaps she had never been so close to one of *them*, and an old one too—I chose not to do so. I actually resolved to let her look her fill, to make no move that might interrupt or deflect her gaze. I pretended to be entirely absorbed by my morsels of grilled chicken. Might she not be gazing at me as Louise Moillon gazed at her apricots, Cézanne at his cardplayers, Van Gogh at his boots, and Rilke at his fountain in Rome?

The grill, opposite the now twilit mosque, was apparently a focus for social events. Two young waiters were polishing glasses, rattling knives and forks, setting a long table for a feast. Sounds from the street: traffic, donkey carts, footsteps; for once, except for a faint throb of electronic drums, a pause in the usual assorted musics. And then, as if from the other end of the world, a derisory cackle, with a hoot for crescendo, broke through these habitual sounds, over and over, while a low voice, provoking it, warbled on and on. The Mona Lisa occupied the one segment of my auditory circle from which no sound was coming; this was also the one and only segment of my visual semicircle into which I forbade myself to look.

There was a good smell coming up from the embers of the fire in the downstairs window frame, where little folded knobs of chicken and lamb chops were being grilled, each run through with a wooden skewer: the stylus, I thought, which for aeons has inscribed into the subtext of Anatolian history the taste of meat. And still I sensed her eyes on me, so I wondered what she was making of him: "Why alone? Where from? Can he speak? What is he looking for here in our town?" I was thinking, too, that downstairs sat another presence. It had loomed up out of a twilight as I had walked in: the silent wrinkled crone who reached out her hand to take your money. For how many years had she sat at her desk in that nook, blinking at numerals? But dovetailed into the deflection of my concern was "his" thought: Who is this being? Does she suffer, that such sidereal spaciousness should contract itself into the gaze she is levelling at me? Does the little boy know what a radiance can break out of the meat of his mother?

Eventually, the Mona Lisa stood up to leave. She walked with a lazy shuffle, haunches swaying, not because she was heavy, but because that was the right way to walk, as if afloat, yet hardly lifting the feet, like a Navajo canyon woman (again, from below, the cackle and the hoot). As she floated down the narrow staircase, following the boy and the husband, I saw her headscarf flutter a little and wanted more than ever to see her hidden face. She kept on walking, shuffle shuffle. I did not suppose that she felt my gaze on the back of her head, as I had for forty minutes felt hers on one side of mine.

That afternoon, at Pisidian Antioch, an hour's busride to the south, I had walked over the outcrop of granite on which masons once constructed a temple of Augustus, to supercede a more ancient shrine, that of Kybele. Now the round Anatolian head of Kybele, enshrined in a nondescript headscarf, had disappeared, surely passing through a puff of wood-scented smoke at the foot of the stairs.

Yet of course we eluded each other, excluded each other. Her gaze, whether aesthetic or sexual, or both, as it were astride those two rungs in the ladder of her curiosity, had been scanning chiefly the right side of my head, and I'd had only a glimpse of her. And though I'd sensed her gaze, its aura, moving around me, I cannot guess to what extent she really fathomed me; besides, my interpretation of her had gone off along a mythical tangent.

Was I, to a woman most likely ignorant of "art" as Westerners mean it, standing in for an art object? Not exactly. Stretch the analogy, even then, and here was a man being studied as if he were some sort of art object, by a person in whom that same man detected a resemblance to a woman immortalized five centuries before by Leonardo's painting. Yes, I had come to know, almost, how it felt to be held under the gaze of the Mona Lisa. Cackle and hoot forsooth! And the circles of analogy had multiplied: in the moment of such an "aesthetic experience" your body has become an antenna for your dead, if you remember them. You have the experience for them, not only for yourself. You have become a feeler extended by those who can feel no more. Through images, with a whole heart, now, if you can, you do invoke them. For the record: as I sat there alone, I recalled a Madonna of the Rocks that presided over the Broadwood in my father's music room, and a Venus Anadyomene—her gaze, not quite focussed yet, would rest on the students who came for tea on Sundays. Her reflection appeared on the silverplate teapot when my mother tilted it.

That steady gaze of the Turkish Mona Lisa—no, I am supplying it, unless, steady as it seemed, I not only imagined but also sensed it—I did sense it by some means supplied by ancient powers she possessed, no marvel to her, powers of sensitive participation. So, even if I supply or not only imagine the gaze, she was unknowingly conjuring out of me a power to match her own. At least, she was animating me to participate in her gaze by interiorizing it.

This was hardly communication; or else it was—subdued and lopsided, but a communication of the isolated, as Montale has described it. If so, had I not got the richer share of it, a hint of "the fatal isolation of each one of us"? Yet what a tenuous space for two beings to hoard their strangeness in—the diagonal across two small tables upstairs in a small grill in a small tattered town, with the enormous material spread of Anatolia on every side; a crushing weight of time, hot lake, freezing mountain, zoomed over, beneath, and around them, while they were secretly moving, moment by moment, across each other's independent lines of perception.

It is no wonder that principally women have challenged any aesthetic grounded in the attentive masculine gaze, wherever it might be directed. Men told themselves that the pictures they studied, poems they recited, spoke back to them in their chilled language, men's, and that a circuit could be completed by such intellectual participation, a judgment of value recorded. The gaze I had felt was liquid, light, calm, circumambient; touching, rather than probing, it reminded me that I had a heart with secret deeps of its own, a heart *in the clear.*

The gaze of the Turkish Mona Lisa, directed at me, her stranger-creature, all unknowingly, and my not shaking it off, but gladly receiving it, not yet recognizing it as a gaze aforetimes feared—called *fascinatio*—combined then to alleviate my doubt as to the resonance of the singular. Yet how mute the singular was, silenced by the cocksure chorus of generalizations. Speak out you must, if only to test the air, to define your opalescence, but who would appoint a paradise under a dunghill? If the use of knowledge was to straighten understanding, wasn't it also to animate it, to lift understanding up, straight off the ground?

Yes and no. Poetic understandings are, leastways, narrow unless grounded: earth means to have her say. They are grounded even in dry areas of knowledge, where only doggèd scavenging may release a trickle of poetry; grounded also—"orphically"—in subterranenous torment. Corkscrew tracks, not straight ones, spell themselves out between you and the mountaintop. But the new Moloch, instantaneous information supplied readymade, cannot accommodate this Turkish Mona Lisa gaze, for the gaze dwells in a mobility that sustains the interval between knowledge dispersed all over the nervous system and the jet of a poetic word. Such a word originates in the *storage*, but its trajectory outside, its own velocity in time, depends on the nuances of its tone and the values that mobilize its freight. Significance, being subject to change, is something emergent, minutely so, something also that disappears as if it were too volatile to be coerced by conscious powers of attention.

When art comes into this puzzle, it could be to show what mortality is not, to explore shimmering borderlands. On the vexed way to what eludes the gaze, it lives untroubled, made strangely of ourselves, across uttermost limits of recital.

Sometimes vaporizing those limits, so that dried-up things can be perceived afresh, pristine, in the condition of their emergence, it is Apollo when art, discharging frenzy, achieves balance. Economics and politics, from that distance, will have shrunk to pinpricks. A simultaneous concentration and diversification of language particles transforms all slack into energy; and the energy is all gaze, all myth, atmospheric, the imaginary, a radiance of the remotest chance to be glad for what you cannot possess, cannot territorialize. Old misery festers, old fear persists, and difference animates an increasingly nervous few. Yet from the gladness we learn not to mistake myth for contingency, and not to mark out, as Adversary or Angel, any other kind of unquelled ego who happens also to be passing by.

These, at least, were my afterthoughts in the night bus travelling south to the sea.

A Postscript to the Great Poem of Time

The poem is about itself, as life is properly concerned to produce, diversify, and maintain, at all costs, life. Of course it is not like music, for it impregnates its subjects, currently, with the illusion that, though massive, it is linear and moves from one point to the next. The poem has a back which it hides; so does a huge snowball. It is no more linear than earth is flat, and it envelops its solar system, in which, unlike a snowball, for its extinction would not be rapid, it has built a nest.

Some of its rambling mutations last longer than others; as in nature, so in the depths of history. Uniquely self-interested subjects having no part in either, browse as they may in such pastures, turn sickened from its crimson blizzards, dazzling chasms.

On its back, then, it carries innumerable spores, which are flung far and wide by its motion, that is to say, by how and where the motion was, before subjects became involved in its rolling. The spores, which include bacteria, have sprung from what was and from what might have been but, inexplicably, failed to be what it had barely begun to be. Atavisms, some mothering splendour, most fathering horror or filially abetting it, erupt among the spores, are conceived and hatched by spores that seem—so swift is eyesight in a mortal span—to have vanished.

Some larger spores resemble globules, multicellular bubbles. These are the "kingdoms" of animals, plants, of any organism among the natural orders. The globules that house living humans are not mistakable for those that house dead ones. Here prosody itself provides markers. Occasionally globules collide, but the living group is articulated in a rotatory syntax (sestinas come into play), the other as anagrams, the rigid anagram substituting for the inevitably garbled but apparently real (and repetitive) speech of the dead.

The poem bounces, at times it breaks off, floats, executes spiralling parabolas. Its leech-like bacterial spores may be ineradicable, though they might come loose. The climates of its feeling, crystallized not only as cases of divorce or mutual rage between nations, are seldom to be predicted, because their variety has no limit. Are there, even then, seasonal promises, glacial Springs, Autumns of fruitlessness?

Certainly the poem smells: of coffee roasting, of a witch's crotch, the reek of ill-nourished galley slaves, of martyrs burning, whiskey-soaked saloons, broken drains (the heady fumes transport teams of spores in track suits by air to stadia in the Caucasus), and pinewoods, the iodine sea-coasts, cordite, and many smells that exist, like ghosts, only in the memory.

The voice of the poem of time is polyglot but no trumpet. It comes, this voice, and it goes. Irregular waves of gravitational force brush it away, storm it out of earshot, return it singing in the bright contralto of a wren. Yet even the apodosis of the sentence it was about to revoke trails off, a snippet.

Into each snippet, however, are built the outlines, now marked, now fading, now gone again, of a waiting room. Over the heads of the multitude inside, stiff in sedimentations or moving about as the travellers strike their antiquated attitudes, the roof lifts majestically and on every side the walls expand, roof and walls perform an immense and constant inhalation, constantly (in the illusion of this idiom, rotatory or anagrammic) the space expands, the furniture dwindles, and it is less and less likely that any transport will ever arrive, for the waiting room is coming to encompass, inescapably, whatever journey might have imagined itself into these multitudinous heads.

So to have read the poem at all is to have read it only at random; but when there is time you can pass it by reading again.

From Depictions of Blaff

The Pines of Rome

When I stood on the Appian Way, says Blaff, among those big umbrella pines and sarcophagi, I was thinking, first, that we should not call them umbrella pines. How dainty, how cautious that is. What words we apply, to diminish the lords of creation. Pine, all alone, pronounce it, breathe it, the word as such spreads and is tall enough. Yet was that thought also picayune?

And then I imagine myself, hearing at long last the wind harmonic in those native pines (never mind the sarcophagi). I was home at last, there, with my tablets and my stylus, there in the rearguard, right at the back of that immense marching army. Scribbling of course, the accounts, you know. These expeditions were very expensive. Money in arrears provoked barrack disturbances. As a colonialist I also felt a qualm coming, but in a wink it disappeared: nobody had qualms in those days.

Oh well, there I was, toddling along, in front of me that great reeking mass of armed men, whichever legions they were, the eagles up ahead, bobbing up and down against the deep blue sky, the cavalry jostling, spears glinting in the sun, wagons packed with paraphernalia, tramp of huge feet in their oxhide boots, breastplates, the plumed helmets, their splendor in the blaze of day, and everyone coming home, home, to the woman, to the children, to your pals in the tavern. So I scribbled to a finish, packed the tablets away.

And took another look at Rome before us: the close-packed city on its hills, stuff of our dreams out there in Britannia, in Gaul, on the frontiers, fighting off those swarms of bog and forest beasts, securing civilization and the laws. But all at once my shirt was whisked off, my tablets snatched away, my worn-out sandals annexed by big strong boots, boots for me too, and my chest swelled in a shining breastplate, I felt the horsehair plume tugged by the breeze flap at my helmet, my sword felt good as it fitted the muscle of my thigh, I held up my head and marched at the front of all my men, my comrades in arms, whose hygiene, whose morale had been for years, three or four, my earnest concern. We had lost many to death. Those who still marched were men who had grieved, and never once had they fought in vengeance, only for the spirit, such spirit as lived in them. We were as one. Wounded, tough, tested, curmudgeons of course; how well we knew life's extreme to middling sweetness.

So with my men, no, correction, so these men, who had depended on me, whom I had not failed, who had not failed their commander either, together we marched, while cheering crowds began to gather, now under the pines of Rome, soon along streets festooned with flowers, where girls stood barefaced in doors and windows waving. With strange shouts and whooping they streamed toward us, our fellow-citizens, wanting to see us, to touch us, and plucking at their mandolins.

This was it. The day never to be forgotten. Our Augustus would be waiting for us, to him, him we would render our salute, as guardians and servants of his Empire. Ah, how qualmlessly we swung along.

The Sycorax Syndrome

Was what Blaff thought as much a mystery to him as to us? Only when finally we left our school did he hold his kaleidoscope still one evening. We'd pinned him down, had we? He said: In three days' time come along after supper with your boundless patience and pencils. Whatever I find to say, you write it out. It won't be long and it's bound to be, I warn you, parochial. Later you can collate your versions and construct, minus my rambling, a coherent text. There were six of us. We never quite knew how or when Blaff got into what he had to say. Shorn of our disagreements as to the relevance of his frequent and funny digressions, here's the gist.

I don't suppose you've heard of the Sycorax Syndrome. I'm not inventing it, only putting a name to a phenomenon. It is a phenomenon of immense magnitude. I name it but can barely comprehend it. Even then, varied as its ancient and present manifestations are, the closer you look into them the more cleanly the name escapes from the purple vapours of "original sin."

In *The Tempest*, Sycorax never appears in person, but Prospero describes her, as a witch "who with age and envy has grown into a hoop." Before her exile on the island and during it, Ariel was her servant, until she imprisoned him in a cloven pine tree. Drawn eventually by Ariel's shrieks, Prospero has liberated him. After wedging Ariel into his cleft, Sycorax became (from "hag-seed") the mother of Caliban. Yet to some interpreters, despite genetic difference, Ariel and Caliban are interdependent agencies of a single authorial spirit: free creative aspiration Ariel, and Caliban "the fury and the mire of human veins." To proceed.

The first two syllables of the name Sycorax derive from the Greek word for fig. Sycophants are people who speak fig—a genteeler turn of speech, wouldn't you say, than sucking up or brown-nosing? As for the last syllable, I note in passing that in German *Rache* (feminine) means revenge, and *Rachen* (masculine) means throat or gorge. It is conceivable that, coming from "Argier," or Algiers, Sycorax was originally a subject of the Ottoman sultan—at least in Shakespeare's time. In Ottoman Turkish, *rak* designates dance or oscillation. *Rakkase* means dancing girl, *rak çarkı* the balance wheel of a watch. These micro-epistemes of circling are only by jocular analogy associable with the potent beverage *rakı*. But here, as Shakespeare divined, is the root of the hoop into which the witch grew with her age and her envy.

The word *envy* also rewards investigation. Could it correspond, in Shakespeare's time, to French *envie*, meaning not envy but desire, or wishfulness? I think so. Possibly it's what came to be called *libido* after Freud. Superannuated libido whirls the witch into a hoop. Though the poor lady's body might have been stooped with arthritis, her soul is a gross malformity. She is vicious, a vitreous and vindictive circle.

That is what happens when the sacred, noumenal sphere of Plato and other Ancients, all the way through to John Donne and Galileo, when that sphere, also celebrated as a sphere of water pulsing in the palms of the true sorcerer, turns into a planilinear hoop, is flattened into a hoop of two dimensions only. Sycorax implies dirty magic, let's make no mistake about that.

So I assign the name to a syndrome which makes, with age and envy or otherwise, a hoop of the human mind. Mind becomes unextendable. Even stretched over painfully limited scopes, mind rolls back on itself. Void inside, no axis to spin on, no spokes to distribute pressure on the rim, the hoop hardens itself, stiffens, till vacuously it implodes, or, at a pinch, it rolls along beside another hoop. For support, it even joins other hoops. In the neural domain, ours, the syndrome shrivels imagination, and thus it obstructs, or shall we say baffles, compassion. It atrophies *caritas*.

Now I must shorten this diagnosis. If I generalize, bear with me. On with it now.

In politics the syndrome is frighteningly noxious. Special interests suck self-interest into their orbit. Vile or well-meaning, politicians are also hooped by specious rhetoric. In the motley world of civil behaviour, narcissists are also afflicted. In the throes of the syndrome's vitreous metastases, a narcissist loses touch with the deeper erotic craving for life by hankering after sex and more sex. Any erotic reality beyond the mirror of prod and snatch carries no weight at all with him. Self-enchantment conceals from him the splendours of sublime imagination, the immense and delicately articulated peacock fan which desire spreads and waves to cool the cosmic furnace.

Catastrophically afflicted are, of course, the terrorists. With no practicable reforms in hand, the terrorist commits, desperately no doubt but indiscriminately, mayhem, for the hell of it or in deadly earnest, sometimes with intent to precipitate an Apocalyptic Transfiguration of Everything. The object is to tempt God—in whichever disguise you fancy him.

Militia groups share this craving for catastrophe. The old Anarchists also plotted for a general blow-up. Some North American militias, so honest investigation has proposed, could be compensating for harm they suffered in childhood. The mask of patriotic hero, the band of brothers hoarding weapons against a day of retribution: similar signs of delusion wrought by the hoop were detected long ago by Dostoevsky and Conrad. History is either too sick, or too unpredictable, perhaps even too magnanimous: a dose of atavistic malice never did procure a pervasive catastrophe or a grand reform of the social scene.

Self-righteous vindictiveness, disgust with externals inverted into self-disgust, and curious degrees of self-deception—these are common symptoms of the Sycorax Syndrome. Vanities of the hoop-mind are found even in placid and polite circles, such as university precincts, not to mention the compounds where Fundamentalists swarm and prate and jump around. Authors too, having spread their wings with Ariel and with gusto, often return to roost on the branches of the syndrome, hoping for applause from Caliban.

These vanities gnaw—how faint the metaphor is—gnaw away the mental aptitudes that otherwise extend beneficially beyond selfhood toward fellow-beings, animals included. They gnaw away till a threshold—of fear? or of brute sympathy?—is crossed. On the far side of the threshold mortality is reduced to victimhood and then to a death-wish.

A hypertrophy of the death-wish or a volitional necrosis atrophies, next, every last impulse of positive desire. But long before this the *envie* will have been paralyzed by *age*, and Sycorax, done with bullying Ariel, will have doomed him to unrelieved agony in a split pine, and incubated Caliban.

Now are these indications novel? I think not. Surely I'm only plagiarizing, unbeknownst, a potential, grave encyclopaedia, *Who's Hoop?* in which varieties of the syndrome across the globe are surgically exposed, while public characters afflicted by it are called to account. There will be, say in economics, indications I'll not make, or only to suggest that fast-growth stock acquisition is right under our noses as a mark of the hoop. False buying power parallels, incidentally, in politics the loosening of power from credible and legitimate authority. The people with most power (like our entertainers) are exposed to the syndrome round the clock, only a little less so people who feel indecently deprived of it. Possibly the syndrome comes into play with the abuse of power. How they grab it, the leaders, unaware that it is a dread and superhuman principle. They fail then to recognize that power is *recursive*. It bites its own tail, it fits the figure of the hoop.

There's red-hot evidence enough that the syndrome has mushroomed at an exponential rate of acceleration during the last hundred years or so, and that the new century is kicking frantically under its spell.

According to optimists, bless them, the spell will only be read backwards when, over a very long haul, damage wrought by centuries, if not millennia, of obtuse economic and social malfeasance can be, if not repaired, then patched up. Others have discerned in the syndrome's present flagrancy (without naming it) an incurable exacerbation of an ordinary wrong-headedness that was baffling humanity ages before the rise of capitalism and, with its dialectical swing, the spread of democracy.

You'll have noticed, here, in my want of proportion, a mark of the syndrome. As its momentum expires, unlike the sphere the hoop reels from side to side, soon to collapse with a clatter. The human sphere, I do believe that rectitude and amplitude of the will is what rounds it and shines it with a sense of proportion. Will you go forth full of radiant life, like other organisms without any will of their own? Will you plunge, as I never did, headfirst into the struggle, to give radiantly intelligent life away? How should I, so marked, speak any truth? Will you search for the truth with vigilance and speak at last of the search?

The Weathervane Oiler

One night in December, the wind rising outside, through the noise of surf, Blaff, the usually taciturn Blaff, who is hunched like a gargoyle on his wooden chair, nodding into the fireplace, quietly admits—"Yes, and to think that once I wanted to be a weathervane oiler." Obviously we asked: "What?" "A weathervane oiler," says Blaff, "someone who oils weathervanes. With a little can of oil he climbs up inside steeples and oils the weathervanes, so they won't get stuck or clatter too loud." "Ah," we say. Aware now that the surf has taken over when his voice left off, we are listening again to the wind as it shakes Blaff's wooden shack on this stretch of terra firma inshore from the dunes.

"That was a good sixty years ago," says Blaff. Chin in hand, he looks around, checking on us: Are we worried? Are we awake? Then he leans back, stretches his legs, heaves a sigh, and speaks again, very softly, but not mumbling.

"It was hardly a vocation, just an idea, and I never did try it out. And pretty soon it was archaeology, another idea, digging deep shafts, a descant to the oiling, down, to complement up. I used to wonder where they'd meet, the way up, the way down. Archaeology was more like a vocation, and I had already scoured whole fields of ploughland, sometimes finding flints." After a long silence Blaff took a sip of the Armagnac and brightened: "Imagine going up the stone staircase from the presbytery, at first the wide ascent, then it steadily narrows, for the steeple proper starts, and then, rung by rung, you climb the iron interior ladder, till the cathedral, or church, spreads out far beneath you. At the top of the ladder, which is raked, by the way, so you have to mount it leaning out and holding very tight, you come to a little door, and you open it. The town is now four hundred feet below you, tiny houses, trees, tinier people in the streets. If it's night, you see the lights twinkling, hear the swish of ravens' wings, their sharp calls piercing the medley of faint fragrances, frying fish, acacia, bonfires, according to season. On a clear day you can survey the shire, much of the island, with all its shires, the mountains, rivers, meadows, towers, castles, perhaps a sea shore? Now comes a difficult bit. You have to sit, just right, on the threshold, lean out backwards and reach up over the lintel coping, and so you grope overhead for the first rung of another iron ladder, the one that's fastened to the slate or stone facing of the steeple. Your fingers find the rung, you take hold, and whisk yourself up off the threshold, grip the second rung, steady your feet on the coping, and haul yourself rung by rung up the ladder. With practice, not so difficult after all.

"There's a can of oil in a holster attached to your belt. then you're at the tip, you reach up and squirt oil into the socket into which the perpendicular rod of the weathervane is slotted, and, reaching up even higher, into the joint where the horizontal bar goes, the one that tells which way the wind is blowing. Then you climb down again. Down again you climb. The last wriggle through the little door is the most difficult bit. You have to angle your body in through the doorway just enough to get a foothold, before you let go the bottom rung outside, on the top rung inside. That done, you take a last fond look at the little worlds that are spinning or twinkling far away down there. I can't say how often you have to oil a weathervane. . . ."

We ask: "What if . . . ?" Blaff grins: "Then you're a goner. Make no mistake." And again he hunches. And is silent. Then again he sips, no, this time he gulps his Armagnac. And he lays a log on the fire. And he is hunched again, his face to the fire.

We have a question; "Were there many weathervane oilers at work in those days?" "I think not," Blaff tells us. Then he stands up. "They certainly were not unionized," he says, "and maybe it was steeplejacks did it on the side, as piece-work, or as recreation? Or perhaps, I used to think, the discipline was too repugnant, nobody did it, and that was why I felt it might be a vocation for me. There would always be work, and you could travel all over the island, get to know all kinds of people, garbage men, itinerant princes, and having selected and trained an heir you could retire with honours and the blessings of an archbishop."

As an afterthought: "Some cathedrals have towers, not spires, towers with a cone on top, easy to reach. And there are many churches, in towns and villages, which have no weathervanes, so you could mount a subsidiary business, installing them. And then what? There could have been artisans, artisans designing complex and subtle weathervanes for me to install. Animals or angels. Swordsmen or saints. Works of art, so indescribable, so high they'd be neighbours to the invisible. As it was, the manufacturers stopped at poultry. Even then, poultry, common roosters might be more resistant to the elements than fabulous elaborate seraphim and whatnot. Just something shining up there, what more do people want? As for archaeology, the less said the better. My discourse is built of my dissensions; but something shining down there—to dig something tangible out was a dull desire, only a diffident nudge from a desire that altered itself as the days flew by. It might have vanished altogether now: a desire to know that down there is where it was."

Again the crash of surf. Heat of the fire. Blaff crouches, hunched again, gargoyle again, on his wooden chair. "The thing might be," he says, "to evolve a mode of knowing that actually takes up into itself the tangible, a subterfuge of domination and so becomes, not as now a little oilcan flourished in the face of the elements, but an all-sufficient element in itself, an agency that quells the rage of what in us corresponds to the elements, namely the distempered will.

"But you see," he now murmurs, "I've been stumbling on a back road of the eighteenth century. Any moment now," suddenly he is pointing to the door as a huge blast of wind buffets it, and Blaff is calling out—"any moment now, one of those terrified starvling poachers will rush in, or a waif gnawing on a stolen cheese rind, and can we hide him?"

["The Weathervane Oiler" concludes the extracts from *Depictions of Blaff*]

Thoreau's Arrow

How deeply into the trunk of the tree had the arrow embedded itself? How high from the ground? How long was the shaft that was still attached to the arrowhead? Did Thoreau pluck the arrow out? Did he only attend to it? Was the arrowhead visible, or did Thoreau only assume that it was lodged deeper in the tree?

What might have been the matutinal thoughts of Thoreau before he saw the arrow embedded in the tree with the shaft attached to the arrowhead? How did he recognize it, notice it was not a twig? How old was the tree? How old had the tree been when the arrow struck it? Had the tree in time expanded around the arrowhead? If so, how much?

What sort of tree was it—soft or hardwood? In what sort of earth were the tree roots embedded? What else might be in that sort of earth? What insects lived in there, and what was their provenance? Did such insects have antediluvian prototypes embedded elsewhere in granite, limestone, or amber? What was the name, what the tribal affiliation, of the Indian who shot the arrow but missed his quarry? What sound did the arrowhead make when it struck the tree?

How many more arrows had the Indian got in his quiver? Did he neglect, still stalking, to extract the arrow, or was it not so precious? Had he made the arrowhead and hefted it into the shaft's tip, or had somebody else done that? Was the arrowhead flint, quartz, or chert?

Was it barbed? Did the Indian not pull it out because the barbs kept it stuck? If not barbed, was the arrowhead oval or triangular? Was it a rabbit point or a point made to penetrate larger quarry, perhaps deer? Elk? Or whitetail?

When Thoreau paused on his walk and saw the arrow, at what stage of development were his thoughts on nature? Did he invent, right there and then, the word *mindprint*? Or was it earlier, was it later? If the arrow stuck in the tree with a shaft still attached gave rise in his mind to the word *mindprint*, which he applied to other such manifestations, what did the new word really signify to him? Was this a discovery of importance regarding the reflective embeddedness of man in nature? Was the arrow for Thoreau a symbol of man's being inextricably embedded in nature, or was it a symbol of man's being vertically equipped to observe a horizon around his embeddedness? Thus *mindprint*, not rabbitprint, deerprint, treeprint, insectprint, not even birdprint?

Did, at the very moment when arrow-in-tree and *mindprint* converged in his mind, Thoreau step outside the mirage of an entirely external nature? Is that question erratic? Stay tuned, can you? Had at that moment Thoreau espied a chink in the fusion of vaporous particles temporarily known as solid reality? Was that chink, if chink it was, something stable to be observed and charted, or was it more like a funnel—conduit? peephole?—opening on the infinite, but a funnel in its fugacity transparent as the wind? Does a person have, therefore, in Thoreau's thoughts, a chance to choose among images of nature, indeed of reality, to which a human mind, given its capacity for chance, conforms only under duress, as one day, after billions more or less idled away, a beast completed a shift of his sensory ground to become an incipient human being? Might Thoreau have figured that certain (and not always fortunate) alignments of chemicals in brain cells can funnel the infinite, like an arrow, even as a quiver of images, into the aleatory twilight branching out behind my conscious behaviour? Was the "chink," even then, more like an immense ache constantly inching through the universe than one sharp cry on Golgotha?

And what extinct organisms, wavering like the voices of certain muezzins unable seemingly to hit the right note, organisms gelatinous or wiry, had laboured to refine themselves into the tree, the arrowhead, the shaft, the sensitive Indian? How much darkness, too, must condense, how slowly, to expel an epiphany? How much heat, cold, dust, moisture, contraction, molecular dancing, does it take to produce one ordinary arrowhead? How much to-do to engender conditions in which a seed may split in the earth and sprout, not exceptionally, one elegant tree?

How many shifting convulsions in a human brain conspire to bring to the tip of a tongue a newborn word such as *mindprint*? How many *mindprints* to pronounce a singularly telling question? How painful must your questions have become to crest in one by which tomorrow the projectile imagination might strike home?

Should we suppose that the tree is called the end of history, would it not follow that, instead of being shot into the living tree, the arrow sprouted out of it, shaft foremost, a reversed Messiah, no Messiah? Is there not stronger evidence that history does not end, has not yet ended, the tree lives, and that the arrow is in perpetual transit, a figure of the spirit?

So have Abraham's actuaries been duped, duped into a panic? Do their shining eyes now promise nothing but a rage for catastrophe still uncommon in the woodlands of Vermont? Has this not happened, time and again, before—when the human claw reaches out to drag down gods from their heaven? Those actuaries, dispossessed and aggrieved, into what corners of credulity have they been driven, that they should propose to lure by carnage a redeemer out of seclusion, as if the smoking flesh of their sacrifices were a bait and the arrow a weapon? As particles of the wood, no mob, no other, can we ever learn to be really here, to take our time, secret or public, not to leave it? How do we print on it a still sporadic track toward a people in whose habitat the tree endures its seasons, but who, having outlived completion of the Fall, may become various and light as birds?

Sources and Notes

Texts come from the following books. (In many cases, writing preceded publication by several years.)

Our Flowers & Nice Bones (1969)
The Lonely Suppers of W. V. Balloon (1975)
Pataxanadu and Other Prose (1977)
Carminalenia (1981)
Serpentine (1985)
Two Horse Wagon Going By (1986)
The Balcony Tree (1992)
Intimate Chronicles (1996)
In the Mirror of the Eighth King (1999)
Crypto-Topographia: Stories of Secret Places (2002)
Of the Mortal Fire (2003)
Depictions of Blaff (2010)

Grateful acknowledgment is made (in two cases posthumously) to Fulcrum Press (1969) and Oasis Books (1985) and as follows: *Intimate Chronicles* was published jointly by Carcanet Press and The Sheep Meadow Press (U.S.A.); *Of the Mortal Fire* by The Sheep Meadow Press only. *In the Mirror of the Eighth King* and *Depictions of Blaff* were published by Green Integer (U.S.A.); *Crypto-Topographia: Stories of Secret Places* by Enitharmon Press. Other titles, mostly collections of poems, were published by Carcanet Press, which also published "Louise Moillon's Apricots" in *The Pursuit of the Kingfisher* (1983), a collection of critical essays.

• • •

"Curbaram": This was prompted by a barbarous Latin text, shown me by Ann Clark in 1967—she was then taking an elementary Latin course with the late Gareth Morgan, classicist of great brilliance at the University of Texas at Austin. For speaker I had Ho Chi Minh in mind. Several bright ideas of Miss Clark's also went into "Manuscript in a Lead Casket," which was written in 1969 or 1970.

"The Birth of the Smile" was prompted by Rilke's fragmentary translation of a poem by Leopardi.

In *Serpentine*, evil was the motif running through twenty typographically peculiar texts.

"The Pines of Rome" alludes to the last part of Respighi's tone poem of that title (which I've always associated with the Via Appia). The speaker, Blaff, is an economist, hence the tablets on which he keeps accounts.

"The Weathervane Oiler": Count Hermann Ludwig Heinrich von Pückler-Muskau recounts in his *Briefe eines Verstorbenen* that while travelling in England during the later 1820s an old man whom he met in Salisbury claimed to have been a weathervane oiler (the count believed him, too). Blaff is here talking to students of his who have known him since they were children (a reader might consider them as "Kabirs" to Blaff as homunculus, but the alchemical context is remote).